ROWAN WILLIAMS

Anglican Identities

DARTON·LONGMAN + TODD

To Geoffrey Rowell
and Kenneth Stephenson

First published in 2004 by
Darton, Longman and Todd Ltd
1 Spencer Court
140–142 Wandsworth High Street
London SW18 4JJ

ISBN 0–232–52527–7

A catalogue record for this book is available from the British Library.

Designed by Sandie Boccacci
Phototypeset in 10/14pt Galliard
by Intype Libra Ltd
Printed and bound in Great Britain by
Cromwell Press, Trowbridge, Wiltshire

CONTENTS

Chapter One

The Fifth Annual Tyndale Society Lambeth Lecture 1998. The full text entitled 'Tyndale and the Christian Society' was first published in the *Tyndale Society Journal*, issue no. 12, March 1999, pp. 38–49. (Rowan Williams is a patron of the Tyndale Society. Further details of the Society's aims, activities and publications can be found on its website, www.tyndale.org.)

Chapter Two

A lecture delivered under the auspices of Corpus Christi College, Oxford in 2000, as 'Hooker the Theologian', to mark the fourth centenary of Hooker's death. Published in *Journal of Anglican Studies* 1.1, August 2003, pp. 104–16.

Chapter Three

Published as 'Hooker: Philosopher, Anglican, Contemporary' in *Richard Hooker and the Construction of Christian Community* edited by Arthur S. McGrade, MRTS (Tempe, Arizona, 1997), pp. 369–83. Copyright Arizona Board of Regents for Arizona State University.

Chapter Four

A lecture delivered for Trinity College, Cambridge in 1993 to mark the fourth centenary of Herbert's birth.

Chapter Five

A lecture delivered at Westcott House, Cambridge in 2001 to mark the centenary of Westcott's death.

Chapter Six

Published in *Michael Ramsey as Theologian* edited by Robin Gill and Lorna Kendall (London: Darton, Longman and Todd Ltd, 1995) pp. 9–28.

Chapter Seven

Published as '*Honest to God* in Great Britain' in the fortieth anniversary edition of *Honest to God* by John A. T. Robinson (Louisville, Kentucky: Westminster John Knox Press, 2002), pp. 163–83.

Chapter Eight
A lecture delivered to a conference on the interpretation of the Fourth Gospel at the University of St Andrews, 2003, under the title 'Anglicans on the Fourth Gospel'.

INTRODUCTION

The question of what if anything holds together the Anglican Communion has recently become a painfully immediate one. The answer will take a fair amount of time to work out; and the essays in this little book are meant to suggest that any answer that is more than just a temporary political adjustment will need to reflect the lives and the ideas (and the prayers) of some of those who, for various reasons, are recognised as in some way credible representatives of Anglicanism over the centuries. Anglicans have always been cautious about laying too much stress on formulae over and above the classical creeds; and that has proved both a strength and a weakness. A strength because it has at best focused attention on the fundamentals of Christian orthodoxy in a way that allows people to 'inhabit' this tradition without too much defensive anxiety about contemporary battles; a weakness because this makes rather a lot depend on the capacity of individual theologians and teachers to orchestrate the central themes of the tradition in a satisfactory way at times when the lack of external norms and boundaries has become a serious worry.

It is not true that there is no distinctive Anglican doctrine. But the discovery of it may require some patience in reading and attending to a number of historical strands, in order to watch the way in which distinctiveness shows itself. The chapters in this book reflect on a number of well-known figures in Anglican history with this in mind; and I hope that some of the connections and echoes will be clear. Of course, there are countless others who could have been examined. The biggest gap in this material is one that is sadly familiar in writing about Anglicanism – the period between the execution of Charles I and the High Victorian age. Given more time, I should have liked to include some study of Thomas Browne, physician and philosopher, Dr Johnson, one of the most serious and in some ways surprising Anglicans of his age, and Bishop Butler, whose philosophical apologetic distilled in very intense form some of the intuitions of an earlier period. But the material here presented has depended a good deal on particular invitations to reflect on particular people, and for whatever reason the names I have mentioned have not arisen. Any unwary reader, then, needs to be warned that the tendency to ignore what Anglicanism meant in this lost period of the late seventeenth and eighteenth centuries is not a healthy one; I hope such a reader will be inspired to fill the gaps by their own exploration (and the recent anthology, *Love's Redeeming Work*, to which I have occasionally referred in these pages, offers ample suggestions).

The word 'Anglican' begs a question at once. I have simply taken it as referring to the sort of Reformed Christian thinking that was done by those (in Britain at first, then far more widely) who were content to settle with a church order grounded in the historic ministry of bishops, priest and deacons, and with the classical early Christian formulations of doctrine about God and Jesus Christ – the Nicene Creed and the Definition of Chalcedon. It is certainly *Reformed* thinking, and we should not let the deep and pervasive echoes of the Middle Ages mislead us: it assumes the governing authority of the Bible, made available in the vernacular, and repudiates the necessity of a central executive authority in the Church's hierarchy. It is committed to a radical criticism of any theology that sanctions the hope that human activity can contribute to the winning of God's favour, and so is suspicious of organised asceticism (as opposed to the free expression of devotion to God which may indeed be profoundly ascetic in its form) and of a theology of the sacraments which appears to bind God too closely to material transactions (as opposed to seeing the free activity of God sustaining and trans-forming certain human actions done in Christ's name).

And on this (I hope) reasonably generous definition, I have presumed to include someone I am increasingly persuaded is the true theological giant of the English Reformation, William Tyndale, although he lived and died before the full and formal breach with Rome. Tyndale's theology, which I have tried to sketch in the first of these essays, is above all a critique of a certain 'professionalising' and localising of religious practice, as a limited territory within human life – capable of being delegated to a priestly caste and reduced to ritual obligation. In place of that, he defines a kind of discipleship which deeply marks later English Protestantism – valuing the home and family as the place where the school of Christ is encountered, seeking not to replace but to sanctify and transform 'natural' allegiances, and, more drastically, assuming that Christian discipleship will change social and eco-nomic relations to an almost unrecognisable extent. Wilberforce's evangelical passion for reform, Westcott's Christian Socialism, Temple's work for the welfare state are all foreshadowed – as are some less happy developments which have nurtured an uncritical attitude to the domestic and the national, and a passive and col-lusive understanding of the Church's establishment.

But it is this urge to break down certain barriers between sacred actions or persons and the social enterprise at large which can also be seen at work in Hooker, with his reluctance to go along with any doctrine of the Church that ties it too closely to a supposed biblical paradigm, when that has the effect of turning the Church into an association held together by human choice rather than divine election. Divine election deals with us ineluctably as members of communities, including the natural communities we happen to belong to; Hooker would have understood at least some of that modern mission theory which insists that we evangelise people *in* and not out of their actual human affiliations. What is distinctive about Hooker – as I've tried to argue here – is that this is deeply rooted in a very carefully worked rendering of the orthodox doctrine of Christ's two natures and his 'inclusion' of renewed humanity in himself. Hooker defines a theological perspective centred on wisdom, the joyful gaze directed towards God the Father through the incarnate and glorified Son, wisdom incarnate. As the second essay on Hooker proposes, we need to see that for Hooker the important distinction is between doctrine that directly serves this definition of our goal as creatures in God's image and various teachings about order or specific controverted points that may be of great significance but do not affect how we see our humanity in Christ.

Hooker's focus on the central mysteries allows him to stand at some distance from a crude sub-Calvinist interest in conscious assurance. His brilliant analysis of this question, which links him so remarkably to the Spanish mystics as well as the Fathers and medievals, needs to be read alongside the way in which George Herbert deals with the same paradoxes and brick walls around assurance and perseverance. Herbert stands close to Hooker – but, as we might expect from a poet, presses still further, implicitly refusing even Hooker's subtle resolution, or at any rate transposing it into a higher and more risky key. It is here that we realise how little this tradition is simply consolatory, how little it has to do with the cultural cosiness sometimes rather misleadingly associated with the early seventeenth century. The spiritual endurance commended and realised by Herbert is not at all a Stoic chill, more of a passionate willingness to cling to an invisible, absent God who is yet the source of all good and joy – an embrace of emotional ambiguity and doubt on the basis of a deep and sophisticated doctrinal conviction. T.S. Eliot's voice is foreshadowed here, as are many of the divided yet faithful minds of Christian modernity.

Herbert's faith requires what has been called a 'passionate patience' (my thanks to Ken Costa for drawing my attention to the use of this phrase in a modern biblical translation). In the essay on Bishop Westcott, I have argued that something like this is what is going on in his biblical scholarship, with its intense focus on

linguistic detail opening out repeatedly on to the widest of doctrinal perspectives. Once again, we have an 'inhabiting' of the
classical doctrinal frame of reference that is serene and confident;
but it sits alongside the willingness to explore every nuance of
what scholarly work can deliver to assist the reading of the Bible.
Westcott's work is echoed very clearly in Ramsey, though here we
also find a more developed doctrine of the Church – one which is
prophetic, I suggest, of some of the great themes of ecumenical
theology in the later part of the twentieth century.

Throughout the tradition up to this point, I have argued, there is
a certain unselfconsciousness about the governing lines of classical
doctrine, a willingness to see these as simply the basic map of the
territory the Christian lives in. If my reading of Hooker is correct,
this is partly a taking for granted of what he argues: credal doctrine
is simply the definition of the human goal in God, by way of the
Trinitarian and Christological dogmas. You can only fully face
the complexities and struggles of individual psychology and of
public and political life on the basis of this agreed framework
describing the human in relation with God. In a less spiritually
alert and a intellectually literate environment, this could mean that
doctrine might become *no more than* a remote framework; a certain
amnesia about the classical idioms and a certain philistinism about
Christian history and imagination might produce a situation in
which the definitive relevance of doctrine had become invisible.
The crisis around the publication of *Honest to God* in 1962 suggests,
in retrospect, that this had indeed happened; the legacy of Anglican
'liberalism' (never a very clear concept) had bifurcated, as suggested in the Westcott essay, into very diverse styles; and Bishop
Robinson attempted to work out more thoroughly than most the
implications of one style. My reflections on Robinson conclude
that his book reflects a genuine loss of nerve in theology; it did
not *have* to happen, but the pressures of the age and its myths
were unprecedentedly heavy. Robinson reinforced one of the most
potent myths of the period very strongly, and the deep ambiguities
of the book have seldom been fully recognised. Readers of Iris

Murdoch's 1966 novel, *The Time of the Angels*, will have noted how the novelist sees, as the theologian did not, how the evacuation of the transcendent God in favour of creative will subjects the human world to the governance of 'angels', agents of inhuman spiritual power, answerable to nothing. This particular 'Anglican identity' is a disturbing one, reminding us of the cultural captivity that can result from a particular kind of establishment mentality. Robinson's own transparent goodness and optimism made him a flawed reader of his times – though a brilliant mirror to them.

The final chapter is a brief survey of significant exegeses of St John's Gospel by Anglicans; it seeks to describe some unifying factors among some of these, and concludes, perhaps surprisingly, that Anglican readings of John have not been universally cast in the mode of Platonist conciliation, light and harmony, but focus quite sharply on themes of judgement and tragedy. There is immeasurably more to say about this exegetical tradition, and its reflection in many other writers – Scott Holland, Dean Inge, Donald MacKinnon, Alan Ecclestone – but I hope that this may suggest further directions. These pages attempt only to confirm what is repeatedly suggested in earlier chapters: that assumptions about the optimism or smoothness of Anglican exegetical and theological method need questioning. There is in the Anglican identity a strong element of awareness of the tragic, of the dark night and the frustration of theory and order by the strangeness of God's work.

So as we try to find a sense of *common* identity among figures like these, we are, I think, driven back to some of the early themes of English Reformed Christianity. God does not belong in a limited area of human life; but one implication of this is that we do not find or identify God with ease. He may be encountered in any area of psychological experience or of political challenge. To recognise him in these unexpected places we need, most certainly, a discipline of scriptural thinking, informed by all the resources that can be summoned in the intellectual sphere, and an inhabiting of the doctrinal tradition that reminds us again and again of what we are for as creatures and as adopted children.

There is little here that can be quickly summarised as utterly and uniquely Anglican – these themes can be easily paralleled in Lutheran, continental Calvinist and Catholic sources. But perhaps there is a distinctive constellation in Anglican history: the Reformed Church of England emerges in revolt against a medieval map of the world in which the Church was in danger of becoming a political entity alongside others; it develops in tandem with a fantastically inventive period in the use of the English language, producing both a profusion of metaphor and a quick, critical sense of the possibilities and dangers of rhetoric; it discovers both a language for Scripture and a Scripture that shapes secular language, so that its biblical fidelity is deeply bound up with a feel for the riches and the traps of speech. The result is a mixture of poetry, reticence, humility before mystery, local loyalties and painful self-scrutinies. It is not a formula for being Anglican; simply a description of how and where some kind of recognisable historical identity came to exist.

Its future is of course unknown, and I have already foresworn any aim to provide a fresh rallying-point for Anglican identity in these pages. But perhaps there is one thing worth drawing out. The writers discussed here in their different ways are apologists for a theologically informed and spiritually sustained *patience*. They do not expect human words to solve their problems rapidly, they do not expect the Bible to yield up its treasures overnight, they do not look for the triumphant march of an ecclesiastical institution. They know that as Christians they live among immensities of meaning, live in the wake of a divine action which defies summary explanation. They take it for granted that the believer is always learning, moving in and out of speech and silence in a continuous wonder and a continuous turning inside-out of mind and feeling.

This is an age dramatically impatient and intolerant of many sorts of learning; and the modern church is not exempt. Perhaps these 'identities' may allow and encourage for some readers a pause for mind and feeling to be reintroduced to 'passionate patience'. Perhaps the Anglican vocation still has this to give to the world, Christian and otherwise.

Rowan Williams

Note

Most of these pieces were composed for academic audiences, and are reproduced with few alterations. I hope, however, that they are sufficiently free of jargon and technicality to be accessible to the non-academic reader. Among many friends who have helped me to understand the historical and cultural background or the theological inwardness of the writers I discuss, especially in the earlier period, I must mention Elizabeth Clarke, David Daniell, Sean Hughes, Diarmaid McCullough, Judith Maltby, Charles Miller and Tom Wright. My thanks to them and to many others among audiences who heard these essays delivered as lectures; and, as always, to Jane and the family.

ONE

WILLIAM TYNDALE
(*c.* 1494–1536)

The Christian Society

Tyndale died praying, 'Lord, open the King of England's eyes'; and much of his polemic takes it for granted that the monarch is the only authority capable of carrying out a full reformation of the Church. We moderns easily misread this, supposing the Reformers to have been 'Erastians', a term that has become so loose in usage that it has almost ceased to be helpful; we suppose that the appeal to the monarch implies a doctrine that the 'secular' power is above the ecclesiastical. But to put the question in that way already presupposes that there are *two* quite distinct kinds of authority, and it was this presupposition that the Reformers did not share. Like Luther – but, arguably, with more clarity and certainly a more radical edge – Tyndale believed and taught that the Christian commonwealth was one. If you had asked him about the relation of the Church to the state, he would not have understood – or else he would have assumed you were a benighted papist, concerned about the legal securities of those who had in the Middle Ages made up the ecclesiastical *municipalitas*, the corporate body of clerics governed by canon law over against the corporate body of the king's subjects. One of the themes of Tyndale's treatise on *The Obedience of a Christian Man*[1] is the need to distinguish the diversity of callings in the Christian commonwealth. The exercise of *rule* in this commonwealth is something quite other than the calling to preach and pastor. Preaching the gospel, he insists (p. 207), involves the whole person; there is nothing left over for the regulation of society, and that must be left in other hands. Thus the pretensions of the clergy to tell monarchs their business are both theologically illiterate and politically dangerous. It is popes and bishops who provoke wars between princes (pp. 186–7). The prince – even the non-Christian prince (pp. 177–8) – holds the place of God as judge in the commonwealth; but it must always be remembered that apart from this role he is no more than a fellow human being, and, if a Christian, simply a brother among brothers. So it is because the prince has the right to rule and discipline the commonwealth that he may discipline the Church. Nothing 'secular' about this; authentic evangelical belief repudiates the idea that an independent entity claiming legal exemptions and rights of interference in the relations between persons in the commonwealth, as it were from outside, can claim to be 'the Church'. This, incidentally, is why Tyndale, in the same treatise, interprets Catholic practice in respect of marriage as an offence against the God-given rights of parents and kinsfolk within the commonwealth: the Church permits marriages on the basis of the consent of the parties alone, and so encourages disobedience to natural familial authority as endorsed by Scripture (pp. 168–9). Similarly, the idea that entry into the clergy or the religious state releases people from servile status is an offence against the good order of the commonwealth, fostering resentment against masters set in their position by God (p. 173).

All this may now seem doubly and trebly strange to the twentieth-century reader. Tyndale may not be an Erastian exactly; but is he not, more worryingly, simply a defender of unexamined patriarchy, of the tyrannous hierarchies of family loyalty and patronage? Well, possibly; but my aim is to uncover more fully what Tyndale thought he was doing, what theological vision underlay these uncongenial views, so as to ask what exactly such a theological vision might have to say that is of continuing value. And I have begun in this way in order to remind us all that Tyndale – again, like Luther – saw his project of reformation as what we should certainly call a *political* one. He is not arguing that people should accept new concepts and no more; he is not expressing the hope, in his dying words, that hitherto unorthodox views should be tolerated by the King of England. He is pleading for a reconstruction of the Christian commonwealth in conformity to the basic commitments of evangelical faith. He is asking – we might say – what a society might look like that took justification by faith as its cornerstone. He does not ask how Christian morality might be imposed upon a 'secular' environment. Rather, he begins by examining what the behaviour is, in respect of God and the neighbour, that naturally flows from the conviction of the causeless, unearned love of God towards us. He assumes that such a conviction inevitably shows itself in the form of an altered social pattern. The modern problem of how social patterns are to be shaped and imagined in the total absence of a shared theological conviction is none of his concern – though I shall want to return to the question of how we might use his insight for our own, infinitely more confused, situation.

The chief source for understanding Tyndale's picture of Christian sociality is not so much the *Obedience*, significant as that is, but his treatise on *The Parable of the Wicked Mammon*. This is a remarkable work in any number of ways. It is a lengthy meditation (more than eighty pages in the Parker Society's edition) on the dominical story of the Dishonest Steward (Luke 16:1–13), encompassing a fresh and profound statement of the doctrine of justification as well as a scathing moral critique of the current practices of ecclesiastical and non-ecclesiastical society in respect of the use of money and possessions. It is perhaps the most powerful treatment of social morality to come from the Reformation era in Britain – more systematic and theologically acute than Latimer's sermons, for instance, and with some strong affinities with the radicalism of Winstanley's Diggers more than a century later. It builds on Luther, above all his *Freedom of the Christian*, but goes well beyond the German Reformer in specific social application. It deserves a far wider readership than it has ever yet gained.

Part of its skill and interest comes from its nimble deployment of a basic paradox. We are delivered by Christ from slavery into freedom; and that freedom is experienced and expressed as indebtedness – not to God, but to each other. This is the fundamental point I want to explore in these pages. Luther's *Freedom of the Christian* had already made the point that the Christian through faith shares the lordship of Christ, and that this lordship must be exercised as is Christ's – in self-humbling and service. God's service to us in Christ is both the model and the motive force for our relation to our neighbour, a 'free, eager, and glad life of serving . . . without reward' (ch. 27). The heart of the argument is that Christ does not perform his works of love towards us in order to achieve something: he is already divine, already in the bliss of the Godhead. His works are the outflowing of what he is. The fact of holiness comes first; good works cannot make you holy, since holiness is always the action of God.

Tyndale begins from the same Christological foundation and the same doctrine of God's uncreated action in the believer. 'Supernatural goodness' (an unusually scholastic turn of phrase for Tyndale) is the sole source of authentically good works. And this supernatural gift is the receiving of God's promise in Christ of his favour. What critics of the doctrine of justification by faith fail to understand is that faith is not a human action ('imagination' or 'opinion') but God's, and is therefore 'ever working'. It renews the whole human subject, making us hungry to do God's will (pp. 50–5). Only as we see this divine working in action, in love and service, can we have any certainty about the reality of our faith: the idea that we could be assured of our faith by any kind of introspection would have been bizarre in Tyndale's eyes. But all this is only really intelligible when we look at Christ. He 'was full and had all plenteousness of the Godhead, and in all his works sought our profit and became our servant' (p. 62). What he does, he does not to gain anything but as the outpouring of his nature.

So 'How can or ought we then to work, for to purchase that inheritance withal, whereof we are heirs already by faith?' (p. 63).

If our works are thus devoid of any thought of advantage gained by them, they are *necessarily* directed to the good of the other. They are not done so as to meet the requirements of God (in the straightforward sense, anyway), as if they could affect God's judgement. God is supremely free, and has given us the gift of his life, his supernatural *caritas*, through faith; so that any notion that we are acting to satisfy God takes away from God's liberty, as if we sought to put him in our debt. The debt that now matters is the debt of love owed to each other; and it is here that Tyndale's interpretation of Jesus' parable shows most originality. In the parable, the dishonest steward is the model for those who make friends for themselves by the use of 'unrighteous mammon'. Why is mammon 'unrighteous'? Not, says Tyndale, because it was unlawfully come by: there is a simple course of action with that sort of money. 'Of unrighteous gotten goods can no man do good works, but ought to restore them home again' (p. 69). No, the problem is the evil *use* of money; and the definition of evil use is the failure to use it to meet the need of another. Tyndale apparently would not have sympathised with Dr Johnson's remark that 'a man is seldom so innocently employed as in making money'; or at least, he would have asked some unsympathetic questions. For, 'In those goods which are gotten most truly and justly are men much beguiled' (p. 70). To have made a profit without apparently injuring anyone leads to the supreme delusion that no moral burden attaches to money so made. Wealth is there for the purpose of making friends, and those friends are, without any qualification, the poor on your doorstep. Tyndale, characteristically, takes the opportunity for a sideswipe at Catholic practice: to use your wealth to endow churches in honour of saints, or even in honour of your dear departed mother, is a serious mistake. *They* are not your 'friends' in the sense Jesus means; you do not need to bring them on your side by relieving their needs. In their day, if they were indeed holy people, they were friends to the poor, and we should be better advised to follow their example than to raise altars to them (a very similar argument can be found in the *Obedience* (p. 171), in connection with the honouring of female saints rather than the imitation of their virtues of domestic obedience). But the poor 'which are now in thy time, and live with thee' are your immediate creditors – so much so that the withholding of your surplus is 'murder and theft' (pp. 66–7).

The righteous use of wealth is thus one of the exercises of Christian freedom, *Godlike* freedom. It is not the payment of any kind of conditional requirement to God, and neither is it simply payment to those we think we are particularly obligated to or those we deem to be deserving. We must be to the neighbour as God is to us. Tyndale refers to Matt. 5:44–45: God distributes his gifts indiscriminately (freely), and so must we. But this presupposes our awareness of the nature of God's gift, our sense of its *gratuity*, its unearned character. 'As a man feeleth God to himself, so is he to his neighbour' (p. 77); and that 'feeling' is the Spirit-given sense of release and causeless forgiveness. 'Where the Spirit is, there is feeling' (p. 78). But this 'feeling' of one's own undeservingness is intimately connected with another kind of feeling: our experience of need met and want supplied opens us to the need of the other, so that the believer 'feeleth other men's need' and '[h]is neighbour is no less care to him than himself' (p. 93).

The argument is more intricate and more interesting than Luther's, although the Lutheran doctrine of works as the out-growth of faith is presupposed at every turn. The awareness, bestowed by the Spirit, of what God has freely done for us reveals to us that the nature of the supernatural love that indwells us is gratuity – the pure act of God (to borrow another scholastic term). Love as it is in God is initiative and bestowal before it is response. Prior to any created event or circumstance, God is active; the miracle of grace is that we are caught up in the same movement of uncaused love. Thus our love never waits upon any outer prompting, never looks for any 'natural' ground in kinship or merit. And this is why also Tyndale can say, in a passage that greatly outraged his critics, that the exercise of supernatural love was not restricted to our fellow Christians.

> When thou hast done thy duty to thine household, and yet hast further abundance of the blessing of God, that owest thou to the poor that cannot labour, or would labour and can get no work, and are destitute of friends . . . If thy neighbours which thou knowest be served, and thou yet have superfluity, and hearest necessity to be among the brethren a thousand miles off, to them art thou debtor. Yea, to the very infidels we be debtors, if they need, as far forth as we maintain them not against Christ or to blaspheme Christ . . . [T]hey have as good right in thy goods as thou thyself (pp. 98–9).

It was a sentiment that embarrassed Tyndale's defenders, if we are to judge from Foxe's awkward gloss, claiming that Tyndale spoke only of apostate or delinquent Christians. This is certainly the meaning of one section of this discussion; but the passage quoted, referring as it does to *the* infidels, cannot refer to anything other than non-Christians; it remains a startlingly bold and clear injunction, echoing at many centuries' remove the observation of Clement of Alexandria (*Stromateis* II.xvi) that Christian love, like God's, is not based upon any mere natural kinship, but is intrinsically a love crossing barriers of all kinds.

This passage also brings into plain focus the importance of Tyndale's view that the freedom of divine love sets up a 'debtor' relationship between every human being: 'every man is other's debtor', since 'love maketh all things common' (p. 95). All human beings have rights over each other's property, in the light of the relations established by God's grace. This is reinforced by another set of implications drawn out from the affirmation of the Christian's share in Christ's lordship. That the Christian is 'lord of all' is asserted in Luther's *Liberty* (ch. 14); Tyndale goes further. 'Christ is lord over all; and every Christian is heir annexed with Christ and therefore lord over all; and everyone lord of whatsoever

[15]

another hath' (p. 97). This is indeed a drastic doctrine, yet it is possible to see how Tyndale deduces it. Each one of us is equally free in Christ, equally possessed of God's initiative of love; and *therefore* each one of us is by theological right the recipient of love – including the practical love represented by wealth – from any and every other, since there is no circumstance that could justify *withholding* love.

But lest this should be read as simply a charter for indiscriminate generosity towards passive recipients, Tyndale is careful to stress that the goal of any specific act of practical charity is to enable the recipient to discharge their own duties and debts effectively. The poor should be 'set a-work by the rich, so that they may obey the scriptural injunction to live by the labour of their hands' (p. 99). The ideal is a fully co-operative society: 'Let every man . . . refer his craft and occupation unto the common wealth, and serve his brethren as he would do Christ himself' (pp. 102–3). The poor cannot be allowed to remain an anonymous mass, but must be assisted to realise their dignity as participants in the freedom God gives. Here Tyndale moves most decisively away from a mere doctrine of *almsgiving* towards the ideal of the Christian society as a pattern of reciprocal action and shared dignity: he could not have been content to see anyone as passive in a community that had been made participant in God's action.

Tyndale rightly observes towards the end of the treatise that he is turning Aristotelian ethics upside down (p. 108): the love of God is not something attained to at the end of a gradual process of ascent through the love of the things of the world, slowly purified by asceticism; all our love is grounded in the prior acknowledgement of the love of God, as 1 John 4:10 makes plain: 'Herein is love, not that we loved God, but that he loved us' – one of those unimprovable phrases taken over wholesale by the translators of King James' commission from Tyndale's version. He is wary of a bland appeal to the cultivation of virtue ('Beware of thy good intent, good mind, good affection') because we must not allow our neighbourly love to be affected by considerations of merit and congruence. Once delivered from the 'possession and kingdom' of Satan (p. 47), we are indiscriminately sovereign over each other's goods and services – and thus always ourselves deprived of sovereignty over our possessions *because* we are sovereignly free in Christ to meet each other's need. It is of course possible to exaggerate Tyndale's distance from earlier tradition (and he has no compunction himself about doing this). Despite his attack on the Augustinian language of an 'order of love', in which a proper self-love holds a pivotal position, his insistence that ethics arises from considering the implications of God's love towards us is actually strongly Augustinian, as is the assumption that love in the Body of Christ is a seeking for the other what one desires for oneself, and a recognition that the good of the other is eventually intrinsic to the good of oneself (e.g. *de trin* VIII.iv ff). Tyndale's repudiation of the idea that faith is a human mental activity has analogues in Bernard's debate with Abelard, where Bernard angrily denies that faith is *aestimatio*, a kind of opinion or judgement (*de erroribus Abaelardi*, iv). And I have noted that distant echo of Clement audible in some of his words about love. Yet overall the impression is of a remarkable originality and breadth of theological thought. It is not at all surprising that this work became a sort of test of doctrinal aberration for the persecutors in Britain in the 1530s – as in the well-known examination of Tewkesbery.

But forget for just a moment the stark specifics of Tyndale and the question of whether or not they represent a viable political programme for the twentieth-century or the sixteenth-century Christian. What is the centre of this vision, and how might it be stated in such a way as to provide at least a foundation for what a modern might want to say about the community of God's people in relation to the wider human community? The first part of an answer may be expressed by saying that Tyndale refuses to contemplate the notion of an 'abstract' individual in Christian terms. As recipients of God's love, we are always already implicated in one another's welfare, and our freedom is always and necessarily bound to the concrete form of service (as God's freedom is in

Christ; you might compare Tyndale with Karl Barth on the mystery of an eternal freedom eternally self-limited by self-forgetting). This is more than saying, in the modish phrase, 'no rights without responsibilities': our 'right' is to experience the whole of our environment, including our economic environment, as gift and grace, as there *for* us by God's bounty; but that includes the immediate recognition that we are likewise there for each other. No one is in a position to separate out rights and responsibilities belonging to individuals in a vacuum, negotiated with each other, balancing awkwardly. The focus is upon the flow of life in which persons participate together. And this means too that there is, theologically, no such thing as what we can call 'abstract wealth', wealth that exists intelligibly outside the context of specific human exchange. Here perhaps Tyndale is Aristotelian to the extent of denying that money has a life of its own; but his denial is based on the conviction that the use of wealth is simply bound up with the movement of love and attention between persons, in *and* out of Christ's Body. The strange anthropomorphisms we hear of capital 'seeking' high interest or low charges or cheap labour would not have made any sense to Tyndale. The wicked mammon is not a kind of agent; we are the agents, in virtue of the agency of God enabling us. The use of our resources is one part of a general process by which we realise the mutual service working in us by the supernatural *caritas* empowered through faith. In *that* sense, we are not masters over our capital; we cannot bend the market to our will and our concern unilaterally. Of the Christian, Tyndale says, 'Let him buy and sell truly and not set dice on his brethren' (*Mammon* p. 103) – a phrase that should surely mean not *wagering* on anyone's labour so as to increase profit. Unsurprisingly, his *Obedience* treatise (p. 201) contains a sharp attack on enclosures and the inflation of rents by landlords – the kind of thing that provoked Latimer's anger, not least in the disastrous days of young King Edward, when the moral integrity of the English Reformation was dramatically and almost terminally lost. Unshared wealth, wealth that is not working for the common wealth, is poisonous.

And in our own time of preoccupation with the burdens of international debt, it is salutary to hear Tyndale baldly redefining the debt relationship with the emphasis upon the *debt* incurred by the wealthy simply in virtue of their wealth (*Mammon* pp. 81–2, 95ff.), and the indebtedness to every other human person entailed in welcoming the free grace of God in your own life.

Debt is redefined because the whole idea of ownership becomes destabilised in Tyndale's scheme. An owner is, almost by definition, someone who enjoys an incontestable claim upon certain sorts of property – an abstract person, in the sense already sketched, someone who can properly draw a line around certain aspects of their lives and say, this is *simply* mine and I enjoy sole right to it. In Tyndale's social universe, there are no such atomised claims; everyone's property is 'on its way' somewhere, away from its present holder or else it is theft. But before we conclude that Tyndale is in this particular an anarchist in doublet and hose, we should note what he does *not* say. He does not think that the primary obligations of persons are to humanity in general; he addresses his exhortation to people already involved in very specific relationships, especially families and households. This is where the *Wicked Mammon* has to be read in tandem with the more obviously 'patriarchal' *Obedience*. The obligations traced in the latter are the obligations of ruler and ruled (see especially pp. 173–88, 202–31) at several levels; and, uncongenial as some of this may be to the modern, the point is that these relations are, for Tyndale, the most obvious and immediate context for the exercise of political virtue. I am not an independent individual addressed by the Word of God, but someone who already has a social identity which includes the duty of obedience to various natural authorities – and, no less importantly, the duty of pastoral oversight towards those whom I command. I owe specific duties or debts in both directions, upwards and downwards, and the radical universalism of the *Wicked Mammon* is in no way meant to displace these.

Tyndale's ideal is not abstract fraternity, a community in which all are equal because all relate 'laterally' to one point. Indeed, you could say that his attack on monasticism and the clerical state as conceived in medieval canon law is precisely an attack on something like an abstract fraternity, a corporation of persons bound together by voluntary rather than natural ties. The monk or cleric or nun has opted out of a God-given order – not only the family but the social order of command and obedience in household and kingdom. The bishop or pope trying to direct the prince, (*Obedience* pp. 186–7, 207) and the servant or bondsman attempting to change his social status by entering 'religion' are equally guilty of seeking to improve on the order of natural society as regulated by God's law in Scripture, setting up bonds and obligations to which natural affinity is irrelevant. Tyndale would fully have understood why the Victorian paterfamilias was so shocked by the revival of convents in the nineteenth-century Church of England. But what stops all this becoming a pure ideology of traditional social power is the assumption that, *because* we are none of us isolated social units, the power possessed and exercised by those who bear rule, in family or kingdom, is not strictly a *possession* at all: its destiny is to be the vehicle of the act of God, passing from hand to hand in the formation of a 'common wealth'.

Of course Tyndale is far from wholly consistent or systematic on these points. What he has done is to bring into focus a political problem that still haunts our discussions. A universalist ideal of justice can leave us with a community of abstract individuals, separate negotiators before the tribunal of universal law; it can lead to precisely the rights-obsessed society of our own age, in which each individual arrives in the social process equipped with a variety of enforceable claims. Because of the number and variety of claimants, social life is a constant adjustment of rival interests; the common good is reduced to an uneasy and minimalist consensus in which nobody is doing too much harm to anyone else. Yet a social philosophy that builds solely on the obligations of kinship and lordship leads to a situation of *corporate* rivalries, the tribalism of competing nations, clans, language groups or whatever. Tyndale does what a Christian theologian should: he recognises that abstract fraternity is a dangerous and narrowing thing (he would probably not have been surprised by the fact that modern revolutions of the left and the right invariably seek to break down both familial and local loyalties); but he also sets out to shock by challenging those local loyalties in the name of the claims of strangers – the 'rights' of the infidel, the one who does not belong, over my own substance and comfort. How any political order might embody this he does not resolve: who has? But he might well give the Christian ammunition for arguing that universal justice entails support for local loyalties and family bonds; *and* that such loyalties cannot be reduced to a private and protected sphere quite separate from public morality. The good family man who operates professionally with ruthlessness and greed would be unintelligible to Tyndale, as would the notion that morality could be transmitted solely by private and interpersonal contact, away from the business of the realm.

His attack on monasticism and clericalism, the medieval notion of the clerical body as a sort of para-state, is typical of the Reformers' tendency to throw out babies with bathwater; like others in the period, he is so concerned to guard against the risks of the abstract fraternity that he fails to see the way in which the New Testament itself challenges the 'obviousness' of familial and tribal belonging. Christ and St Paul alike assume that the community of the new humanity may cut across 'natural' belonging, in family or polity, and that these loyalties are capable of seriously interfering with the reconciling work of the Kingdom. The firm hand pushing us back towards the sovereignty of 'natural' communities suggests a striking short-sightedness (from our perspective) about the corruptions and tyrannies of family and state. In the wake of the Third Reich and its pseudo-Christian apologists, we are bound to look less kindly on this monolithic (however benign) patriarchalism and to see more clearly the need for some sorts of institutionalised counter-communities. By the end of the reign of Tyndale's earthly king, whose eyes were certainly not opened in any of these ways, many of Tyndale's allies would have had good reason to feel some scepticism.

And perhaps it is the same excessively tight focus that might make us uncomfortable with the robust denial that we can properly count the communion of saints or the faithful departed as 'friends'. If you remember, Tyndale attacks the use of wealth to endow churches and masses honouring the saints or devoted to rescuing souls from Purgatory. Wealth must be used to make friends; and the departed cannot stand to us in that relationship. Again, the solid immediacy of the community here and now, the poor at the gate, overrides the idea that there might be other kinds of belonging, less tangible and manageable. Tyndale's insistence that the present needs of the poor always 'trump' the desire to honour the dead, because the dead do not need what we can give, is unanswerable; but it succeeds in pushing away the question of what kind of exchange between dead and living might be imaginable within the Body of Christ. Tyndale here is part of that highly ambivalent trend in reformed religion in the sixteenth century which effectively encouraged people to regard the departed as no longer members of the community, a trend whose complex social and imaginative results have been charted by several historians of the age. It is as if, in defending the priority of the concrete community here and now, Tyndale introduces a kind of abstractness elsewhere, in our thinking about the wholeness of Christ's Body across time.

In sum then, Tyndale's Christian society has some searching questions for us about how we understand justification, ownership, lordship, debt, duty and feeling. He protests about doctrines of human solidarity that level off the diverse kinds of belonging that are simply given in our social existence, and warns the Church against a universalism that flattens all our relations into the form of a notional fraternity. Above all, he sends us back to the foundation of our faith – especially those of us who, whatever our qualifications and queries, still stand in a reformed tradition: how does our thinking about sociality and authority reflect or fail to reflect our belief in justification by faith? Good questions all. But there is one final point worth underlining, though it is not one that Tyndale himself makes. He spent his greatest energies in framing a vernacular language for speaking of God – or rather for God to speak. He is searching for words that will be capable of being owned by the poor and dispossessed as words of promise and of transfiguration. By common consent, he achieves a vigour and a music in his work as a translator which no one has really rivalled in our language. And I should want to say in conclusion that the best testimony to his vision of communities and relationships that are not abstract or formal is the language he heard and wrote. He does not write for rootless individuals but for persons with flesh and history. The Bible is no record of God's will for abstract fraternity but the story of peoples and families working justice in their concrete situations and finding universal vision only through the specifics of local and particular callings. And therefore it needs in translation a language that can be spoken confidently aloud by actual persons who live by the rhythms of the breath and the temperature and who address one another familiarly. One of the reasons we are so bad these days at the language of scriptural translation and the language of liturgy is, I suspect, the terrible and false universalism of global culture and atomised humanitarianism, our peculiarities smoothed out by the promises of a universal distributive justice and (what in fact sits very awkwardly with the former) a universal set of consumerist goals, homogenised objects of desire the world over. Our speech betrayeth us. Not the least of Tyndale's gifts is to remind us what angular and particular persons sound like when they are praying, arguing or wooing. Christian society needs a Christian language. Those concerned for Tyndale's language do well to remember what it serves; and those inspired by Tyndale's social vision need to learn how to speak with vigour and honesty about it, in a world of easy and glib speeches.

TWO

RICHARD HOOKER
(1554–1600)

Contemplative Pragmatism

RICHARD HOOKER BELIEVED (injudiciously, in terms of his reputation and career) that Roman Catholics could go to heaven; he believed this, so his notorious sermon of 1586 explains, for what are in fact sound Protestant reasons. Our righteousness is always flawed, one way or another: although the perfect, active righteousness of God works on us by accepting us freely in Jesus Christ and guaranteeing the possibility of full forgiveness, that 'inherent' righteousness which concretely makes us holy here and now, our own appropriation of what God has decisively done, is precarious and unfinished. 'The best things we do have somewhat in them to be pardoned . . . We acknowledge a dutiful necessity of doing well, but the meritorious dignity of well doing we utterly renounce' (pp. 493–4).[1] We cannot in any way put God in our debt. But if sanctifying righteousness is connected with the faith by which we appropriate God's sovereign and perfect righteousness, imperfect righteousness and imperfect faith go together. Hooker elaborates this in his sermon on 'the Certainty and Perpetuity of Faith in the Elect', delivered around the same time in his ministry in the Temple as the great sermon on justification: 'It cannot be that any man's heart living should be either so enlightened in the knowledge, or so established in the love of that wherein his salvation standeth, as to be perfect, neither doubting nor shrinking at all' (p. 471). To make salvation conditional upon a full and flawless apprehension or articulation of faith is thus to undermine the central Reformation principle itself, the priority of God's active righteousness.

But Hooker has another, less obviously Protestant, element in his argument in the Justification sermon. Christian life is a lot more chaotic than his Puritan adversaries might believe: Christian laypeople do things without necessarily assenting to the heretical doctrines underpinning them in the minds of teachers and theologians (p. 498); the mass of believers are unlikely to understand the points of popish sophistication, even if they are aware of them, which they probably aren't (p. 499). What the ordinary Christian holds may well be what Hooker likes to call the 'foundation' of faith, even in a Church that officially commits itself to error. Of course there are deplorable consequences to false belief,[2] but God's mercy is well able to triumph if the foundation remains and is not deliberately rejected. And this means that mutual recognition as *Christian* is still possible between churches that are engaged in radical controversy. A church may be putting any number of obstacles in the way of the sanctification of its members, and it is the duty of other churches to point this out; but this is rather different from a church ceasing in all respects to be a church (pp. 514–15).

Both these points in Hooker's sermons of the 1580s take us close to the centre of his theological method; it is no accident that these were the texts that precipitated him into the hard labour of theological controversy and brought him to the attention of patrons in high places. Both perspectives help us read, perhaps with new eyes, some of the apparently more abstruse sections of the *Laws*, so as to grasp how his commitments in Christology and eucharistic theology and his controversial positions in the politics of his day belong inextricably together. His insistence that faith cannot be 'perfect' in the sense of self-consciously complete and exact (and we might think of the famous remark in Book I of the

Laws about silence as our safest eloquence – I.2, p. 201) is not at all a post-Enlightenment agnosticism in Shakespearean dress, but a recognition that contingent circumstance, human error and sin, and the instability of our personal passions and sensibilities all shape what we think we believe in ways that should make us very cautious about at least some of our claims. In effect, he is perhaps the first major European theologian to assume that history, corporate and individual, matters for theology; and he is one of the inventors of that distinctive Anglican mood which I have elsewhere called 'contemplative pragmatism' – a mood that embraces a fair degree of clarity about the final goal of human beings and the theological conditions for getting there, but allows room for a good deal of reticence as to how this ought to work itself out and scepticism as to claims that we have found comprehensive formulations. The self-critical element in theological formulation here comes not from any strictly *epistemological* uncertainties but from the conviction of finitude and sin, intensified by a quite orthodox Reformed pessimism about human capacity.

But the important insight for reading Hooker on Christ or the Eucharist is the implied, and sometimes explicit, appeal to the priority of divine action. Theological truthfulness is not fully at our disposal because holiness is not fully at our disposal; thus theological truthfulness, while genuinely, even painfully desirable, cannot be deployed as a condition that can confidently be managed so as to determine the limits of the true church. Naturally, churches working in history make and must make disciplinary decisions and enforce them; but they cannot, in so doing, claim to pre-empt divine decision. The Church exists and is sustained by God's action, not by human consensus. This has some crucial implications for how the Church actually works and speaks, and it is these implications that are under discussion in Hooker's treatment of substantive doctrinal matters. In this chapter, I should like to examine briefly some of what he has to say about Christology and the Eucharist in Book V, in order to suggest how the governing themes of these discussions connect with the apparently more *ad hoc* reflections of the early sermons. I shall be arguing that in directing our attention to both contingent history and the present complexity and variety of the believing community, Hooker is in fact making a basic theological point about the priority of divine action; so that, as I've hinted, it is the very notions that prompted accusations of Catholic sympathies which are most strongly rooted in the concerns of the magisterial Reformation.

In the fiftieth chapter of Book V, Hooker begins a substantial exposition of sacramental doctrine (and defence of sacramental practice as received in the Church of England) with an apparent digression on the doctrine of Christ (51–6). Sacraments exist to further our union with God; and that union can't be discussed without discussing its foundation in the union of God with Christ. 'It seemeth requisite that we first consider how God is in Christ, then how Christ is in us, and how the Sacraments do serve to make us partakers of Christ' (51.1, p. 220). There follows a beautifully lucid summary of patristic Christological teaching, designed to bring out as fully as possible the fact that the incarnation is not an isolated fact about Jesus but the ground for a renewing of the entire human race. A renewing, not a total alteration of human nature: Hooker is careful (53.2, p. 228) to steer us away from the idea apparently implied in a passage from Gregory of Nyssa, that humanity is somehow dissolved in divinity, losing its integrity in the process. And we are not to lose sight of the fact that Christ takes to himself in the incarnation 'loss and detriment' (54.5, p. 234). The incarnation so associates God with the human condition in its frailty that humanity exhibits what Hooker calls the 'effects' of divine action in itself, without losing its natural properties; and likewise in those who are associated with Christ, these effects may be realised without the destruction of humanity as it actually is (55.5, pp. 234–5). Hence it is extremely important for Hooker to deny the Lutheran notion that the humanity of Christ in its glorified condition becomes omnipresent (a theory which is developed to make sense of Lutheran eucharistic doctrine): having taken an actual human body, the second person of the Trinity is for ever united to a *specific* material thing which has endured a specific history (he notes the 'scars and marks of former mortality' in the risen body as described in John's Gospel; 54.8, p. 237). As Hooker elaborates this, he repeats the point he has already made about the union that takes place in the incarnation: there is no merging of natures, but there is an absolute continuity and inseparability of action and effect, since one personal agent only (the second person of the Trinity) is acting. We as united with Christ are not 'activated' by the divine person in the same way, but through our union with him in his mystical body, the Church, we can still say that he acts with and in us in such a way that the 'effect' of God follows from what we do.[3] Body as well as soul, we are worked upon by the Holy Spirit in such a way that new effects appear, in many 'degrees and differences' (lvi.10, p. 253); Christ comes to life in us in various ways precisely as the effect of divine action is received into the created self, in its material and mortal condition.

Christ acts upon us and in us through our association with him by the gift of the Holy Spirit. If the point of the incarnation is to restore humanity, the relation we have with the humanity of Christ cannot be a merely formal sharing in human nature; it is a relation with a humanity itself already transfigured (and not annihilated) by the outpouring of divine gift. Anything less is, says Hooker, 'too cold an interpretation' (56.7, p. 250). And this model of union in effect and act is precisely the vehicle Hooker needs to take him through the complexities of debate over the presence of Christ in the Eucharist. In 67.5, he returns to the language of 'effect' to offer a new perspective on the Eucharist: bread and cup are the appointed means by which certain results will follow, namely our renewed participation in the glorified human activity of Christ, and so may be given quite properly the name of the effect they bring about. 'For that which produceth any certain effect is not vainly or improperly said to be that very effect whereunto it tendeth' (p. 352). It is not, he goes on, that Christ's presence needs somehow to be 'in' the bread and wine before we receive them;

the bread and wine are the vehicles of Christ's action to make us partakers of his life, and any further analysis of how this might be supposed to happen is at best irrelevant and at worse impious (p. 353). Papist error about the Eucharist is less in the doctrine of transubstantiation as such than in the insistence on this as the only legitimate account of how Christ acts. It is, incidentally, worth comparing Hooker here with Herbert's poem[4] on the Holy Communion in the Williams manuscript (a long unpublished manuscript of Herbert's poems), which makes much the same point; the purpose of the Eucharist is the transformation of *us*, not the bread. Hooker can say, boldly, that 'there ensueth a kind of transubstantiation in us' (67.2, p. 358); Herbert argues that Christ died for humanity, not for bread, so that it is the former that needs changing – though, again, as for Hooker, without being destroyed in the process. As, in the classical doctrines of analogy, a designation may be given to something in virtue of the effect it produces (a healthy diet, to use Aristotle's famous example), so in the incarnation (you can speak of the incarnate Jesus as God, even though you will recognise that the human individuality of Jesus is substantially unaltered) and so in the Eucharist and the lives of believers. Receive the gift of divine action and the effects of divine action follow – in Christ's humanity, in the bread and wine, in the holy person.

These relatively technical matters may seem some way from the issues with which we began and from the context of Hooker's main controversial agenda. In fact, the connection is clear, and is spelled out by Hooker earlier on in Book V (57), when he emphasises that the purpose of sacramental action is not simply to be a kind of 'teaching aid', supplementary to the proclamation of the Word. If sacraments are indeed a form of visual teaching, it is, he says, all too easy to slip into the assumption that they are a bit of an afterthought, less deserving of reverence and attention than verbal instruction. It also follows, if such a view is held, that there is no point in administering sacraments to children, whose capacity for instruction is so much inferior. In response (57.2, p. 256),

Hooker lists various elements of significance in sacramental practice that cannot be reduced to instruction in any straightforward sense; these are still largely to do with the subjective appropriation of God's grace[5] but he moves on to the simplest, yet most comprehensive justification of sacramental action. The outward act signifies a gift of God which remains invisible (as in the Prayer Book Catechism, of course), but is bound to the execution of the act; sacraments are 'moral instruments, the use whereof is in our hands, the effect in his' (57.5, p. 258). Once again, the favourite word, 'effects': acting with God and under God's instruction, human beings perform finite actions that allow divine causality to be more directly at work in the world without ceasing to be finite actions.

But bound in with this is the assumption that straight ideological instruction is not and cannot be the primary point of worship or the means of growth in holiness. Turn back a little further (V.38), and you find the celebrated *laudatio* of musical performance in church in terms of how music represents to us the life of the passions.[6] Just as the recitation of the psalms allows us to express our variable emotions (37), so music of any kind in church shows us how our affections may be clarified and educated, made plainer to us and converted or confirmed or both (pp. 160–2). Furthermore, the antiphonal pattern of recitation or singing, minister and people answering one another, becomes a powerful sign of the same education of the affections: it shows our awareness of 'our common imbecility', our need for each other's prayer and charity, a readiness to 'wish reciprocally each other's ghostly happiness' (p. 164), and in this way moves us deeper towards true devotion.

In other words, public worship deals with the whole of that humanity assumed by Christ, its frailty and physicality. We are to be concerned about something more than ideas in worship because the act of God in Christ is more than the conveying of information to us; it is the renewal from within of what is possible for human experience. This is the hidden action of God beneath the generally unbroken surface of the world's processes. The detailed Christological discussions, with their insistent exegesis of the Greek Fathers, turn out to be quite substantive controversial moves for a theologian determined to challenge the assumption that 'biblical' worship is necessarily dominated by preaching, to the point that validity cannot really be granted to a sermonless liturgy. What is more, rather paradoxically to our ears, the greater involvement of the congregation in the liturgical process becomes a way of affirming the priority of divine action in the event of worship. The instruction-focused liturgy assumes all too readily, in Hooker's eyes, that accurate information can be satisfactorily conveyed to those in need of it by an ideological specialist; and so it naturally works with a model of the church community which presupposes that you can identify adequate and inadequate levels of under-standing and draw your boundaries accordingly. And this is precisely what he has challenged in the sermons of the 1580s with which we began. A congregation applying strict and clear standards of acceptability for its members stands in danger of two major errors which would undermine the classical Christological synthesis Hooker takes for granted: it would allot no *practical* significance to Christ's assumption of a complete humanity which is then transfigured by the gifts received from the Father, and it would leave no intelligible room at all for sacramental practice, since it would effectively ignore the fundamental repeating pattern of divine action as revealed in the incarnation, created events that carry the effects of divine decision and initiative. For Hooker's opponents, as he interprets their concerns, sacraments could only be human actions designed to further the homogeneity of that community of uniform spiritual achievement which is the holy congregation. To affirm the possibility of uneven, confused faith, even the confused ecclesial loyalties of the 'church papist' (V.68.4–9), as something acceptable within the reformed congregation is entirely of a piece with the defence of a liturgy that is more than verbal instruction; both concerns may be traced back to a Christology which is centred upon divine gift and onto-logical transformation, and a consequent sacramental theology which affirms the hiddenness but effectiveness of divine presence and work in the forms of our ritual action.

In an outstanding recent article,[7] the Renaissance scholar Debora Shuger argues that the overall effect of Hooker's polemic in these areas is to intimate the possibility of a community more unexpectedly egalitarian than we are inclined to associate with his writing. While he has little or nothing to say about the Church as a community in the sense we are rather sentimentally inclined to give to the word these days, a group consciously united by deep fellow-feeling and friendship, while he evidently believes that the Church is a body in which coercion is not inappropriate and looks to the state to provide this, he makes a powerful bid for imagining a sacred community in which the effective furthering of the community's goals does not depend upon the successful manipulation of the community's express beliefs by the work of an elite. Shuger is reacting to a prior reaction in Hooker studies – the revolt, led by authors such as Cargill Thompson and Eccleshall, against the somewhat saccharine portraits of Hooker common in Anglican scholarship up to the 1970s. The preternaturally mild and detached saint of Walton's account was displaced by a shrewd political journalist, perfectly well able to see the advantages of a rhetoric that claimed distance, detachment and tolerance, and an appeal to reasonableness that culturally disenfranchised opponents rather than meeting them on level ground. Shuger's contribution is to point out that, while Hooker is unquestionably a shrewder rhetorician than was once realised, and not quite as otherworldly as his allies would have us believe, nonetheless the reductive political analysis of his work itself accepts uncritically some exhausted and banal paradigms in its account of the political confrontations of Tudor England, and indeed political confrontations in general. Class struggle, the battle for cultural and social hegemony, is complex; it is seldom a plain standoff between rich and poor, elites and masses. Shuger argues that there is another necessary polarity in analysing cultural struggle, that between mythic, traditional and (normally) very material modes of making sense, modes associated commonly with 'the people' at large, and the analytical styles of a class that has 'escaped' from myth and tradition (pp. 324–5)[8]. What this latter class regards as emancipatory is likely to be deeply opposed to the narrative and affective discourses of a wider population; so that the apparently innocent project of emancipation becomes itself an arena for battle between elites and masses, contemptuous rationalists struggling to impose something upon 'lower orders' who habitually communicate and makes sense in other terms.

What I have argued here so far is by way of being an extended footnote to Shuger. Hooker sets up his central theological arguments so as to give some clear privilege to certain themes that might – in a non-pejorative way – be called mythical. The governing narrative of incarnation is developed in such a way that the focal unifying point of the Christian community becomes something both invisible (the prior act of God in renewing humanity in Christ) and extremely, even crudely, material and pragmatic (the conforming congregation at worship in the local church, sitting fairly light to some sorts of doctrinal homogeneity – some, not all, otherwise the central rationale of the Church as Christ's Body would be evacuated of content). Shuger's essay concludes by relating this element in Hooker to the unsettled environment of post-Reformation English society. If global Catholicism no longer provided the defining limits of Christian belonging, what should replace it? The state was ready to step in, and in many respects Hooker is content that this should be so. But upon what base does the state act? Hooker's opponents wanted this to be a pure Reformed theological system, shaped by clear biblical teaching, enforced by godly magistrates of approved orthodoxy. Hooker, as Shuger says, accepts neither this potentially totalising perspective nor a purely positivistic account of the state's authority in matters spiritual. Hooker's congregation is not simply a department of state, controlled by the 'command structure' of Tudor England; it is a community whose goals are clearly 'supernatural' (i.e. the vision of God) and whose social bonds are neither political loyalty (though that is a desired outcome) nor common sentiment, but participation in a 'commonality' of usually not articulated experience rooted in the gift of new humanity by God. The expression of those bonds is through ceremonial actions that both 'put us in the way of' divine activity and make us (conscious or unconscious) carriers of that activity, secondary causes of divine effects.

'Early modern religion typically both creates and occupies spaces outside the jurisdiction of the state. Its various mystical bodies colonize the interstices of polity, erecting international, local, and vertical "societies of souls".'[9] It is in this sense that Hooker's church is an 'imagined community', not just the creature of political coercion. Shuger refers us back to Tyndale at one point in her argument,[10] and there would be a great deal more to be said about how one consistent strand in the English Reformation, perhaps more than in many of its continental parallels, has to do with the inseparability of ecclesial reformation from social reconstruction, a re-imagining of social relations, the sort of thing spelled out so eloquently by Tyndale in his *Wicked Mammon* treatise in particular. The state becomes neither sacred nor neutral, but a conversational partner in the effort to define a satisfactory human life, a partner always *to be* persuaded. At this level, so Shuger says, Hooker is doing very much the same thing as his Puritan interlocutors, who are also engaged in the struggle to persuade the state; but he, by deliberately refusing to tie the Church's coherence to ideological unity (and by deploring, as in V.lxviii, any effort to establish the subjective level of the communicant's orthodoxy or spiritual fitness), gives central place to the cardinal Reformed principle that God is never to be thought of as passive or reactive in respect of humanity's doings, so that the unifying power in the Church remains radically *inaccessible* to state and visible Church alike. We can only work with and from those 'effects' of God's action that appear in conjunction with events in this world – the unique humanity of Jesus, the sacraments, the lives of holy people.

This is where the strangely 'egalitarian' implications of Hooker's theology come to light – though the term is an awkward one if pressed too strictly. Knowledge of God is not dependent upon theological exactitude of the kind the Puritans work for; thus the mythic and ritual life of the 'ordinary' Christian is defended – even though Hooker, like a good Reformed writer, insists that it is subject to severe criticism and pruning when it positively undermines the central themes of a theology of divine freedom, or simply colludes with our unreconstructed passions (we might look again here at his passages on music and the undeniable possibilities of its corruption as a vehicle of devotion). It adds up at first sight to a fairly 'cool' account of communal identity, stressing the solidarities that are not chosen or planned over those that represent clear common belief or feeling – but also removing the communal identity from a simple hierarchically enforced conformity. 'Egalitarian' is a problematic word here, since Hooker would have had no truck with this as a positive account of what he believed; but we might at least say with some justification that his endorsement both of rituals of reciprocity and of popular non-conceptual elements in religious practice works against both a simple divine command theory of visible authority in the Church and the privileging of a theological elite.

And of course it works *in practice* in favour of the existing authorities of Church and state at the particular point of writing. Shuger's demonstration of the resourcefulness of Hooker's imagining of community is wholly compatible with the honest recognition of the specific political goals he pursues. But Hooker himself might have referred us back to his programmatic views on faith and righteousness: a theology may be marked by political ambiguities as part of its confusion and inescapable involvement with the fallen mind, and yet establish a frame of reference capable of transcending all this. His attempt to take his readers to the 'foundational' issues that concern the nature of redemption through the incarnate life is at the very least an attempt to bring his own argument into the light of a doctrinal perspective uncoloured by contemporary church politics, and to submit the argument to this criterion.

One can see why, as Conal Condren has very expertly shown,[11] Hooker's authority owes not a little to the enthusiasm of Catholic controversialists in the seventeenth century, who were very ready to appeal to his defence of the traditional or 'mythic' as an unexploded papist bomb on Anglican territory. Yet, as I have tried to suggest here, any controversial advantage to be gained from Hooker's cautious defences of tradition and usage is substantially offset by the genuinely Reformed emphasis that underlies the whole, the appeal to the priority of divine action as the true locus of unity for the Church. Hooker's crispest polemic against the Roman Catholic position tends to come in circumstances where he can allege that Catholics seek to bind the unity of the Church too closely to formulae of doubtful authority or antiquity. The problem with transubstantiation, for him, is not the supposedly blasphemous or idolatrous implications of the doctrine (though he believes it to be wrong, and seriously wrong) so much as the imposition of a secondary hermeneutical refinement as a definition of essential conformity. Here is a doctrine, he says in effect, that presumes to supplement the fundamental Christological witness to the prior activity of God in redemption: *God* has defined what it means to be a believer by the fact of the incarnation, and no human power has the liberty to add to that definition. Attempting to do so undermines rather than confirms the credentials of ecclesial authority. Hooker's Roman sympathisers in the seventeenth century largely missed this dimension in his work of self-critical or self-checking reference to Christology, and thus missed the importance in his theology of the principle of God's hiddenness in the act of revelation, a hiddenness that secures divine freedom.

Suddenly Hooker begins to sound alarmingly like Karl Barth. This isn't entirely fantastic: Barth certainly insists that the unity and the structures of the Church cannot be bound to human institutions and constructs, and grounds all that can be said of the Church in his fundamental theses about the freedom of God in

Christ. But Hooker, as we have seen, takes the argument off in unexpected directions. Instead of adopting a radical indifferentism about church order such as many have discerned in Barth, he uses the appeal to prior divine action as a dissuasive against any ecclesial reform that treats history as indifferent. There is some presumption, at least, in favour of received forms of church order; to deny this is both to set up a contemporary theological theory as arbiter of ecclesial acceptability (and thus to take a purely human initiative in determining the boundaries of the Church) and to put into question the incarnational pattern of God's invisible self-association with the complex interlockings of human experience – God's working through the links we are hardly aware of, historical and communal, so as to bring us to our perfection. To the Catholic challenge that, on such a basis, there could never be adequate reason to deny the necessity of the papacy, Hooker would reply that the problem comes precisely with a declaration of the *necessity* of anything beyond the basic grammar of incarnate divine freedom. It is perfectly consistent for him to defend episcopacy against Puritan attack on the grounds that there is no prescribed church order in the New Testament and that no order could in any case be so essential to the maintenance of orthodox faith that its presence or absence determined whether or not a body could be a church. Episcopacy is not straightforwardly of divine institution (a conviction which always made his Tractarian admirers uneasy), but it is a reasonable and defensible self-disposition of the Church, originating in the immediate wake of the apostles. That the orthodox faith has been consistently proclaimed in an episcopal church (above all in the formative age of doctrinal statement, the first five centuries) suggests that God's action is not impeded by this structure; whereas (he would probably argue, like most of his circle) the full-blown development of the papacy *does* confuse and obscure the central principle. It is almost that episcopacy is the more desirable the less you think about it theologically . . .

This is not at all a simple issue in Hooker and in his theological legacy, but it illustrates how the criteria with which he works are neither purely opportunistic nor purely ideological. He helps us very little on a question such as whether bishops are essential to church order in the abstract: he simply says that, here and now, bishops are part of the pattern of historical and traditional belonging which shapes Christian identity, so that it is sillier and more damaging to abolish them than to retain them. There is no clear evidence that they are a mistake, at least to the extent that they have not stifled the orthodox witness to the Word incarnate and provide a sensible context of discipline and validation for sacramental ministry (whether or not, once again, that is in the abstract the only imaginable context). The removal of bishops assumes that we have access to the mind of God valid for all time, through the pages of Scripture, on a matter whose connection with the saving transformation of our nature in Christ is remote. Better to trust our history where it does not appear actively to mislead us.

By now, you will have some flavour of just how paradoxical Hooker can be in his arguments. Tradition, the discourse of the non-elite or less literate, is defended on the basis of the same Reformed theological method that campaigned for the open Bible and Christian literacy. The rights and liberties of the laity are affirmed by way not of a defence of scripturally based debate but with a spirited denial that truth is discovered by any kind of detached or non-historical reason. The desirability of bishops is insisted upon by refusing to argue their theological necessity. It explains why Hooker's appeal has never been a narrow one, in or out of Anglicanism, and why he cannot be represented (certainly in the light of recent scholarship) as either a pure conservative or a doctrinal indifferentist. I refer back to the designation of 'contemplative pragmatist' for him: he is pragmatic to the degree that the accumulation of historical precedent has real intellectual weight, in the light of our ineradicable folly, selfishness and slowness as human thinkers, and he is contemplative to the degree that his guiding principles are seen by him as received, not invented, as the uncovering of a pattern of 'wisdom' in the universe, focused in and through the Word incarnate.

His Christology allows him to imagine a church of a certain kind; contemporary ecumenical and systematic concerns press constantly for something 'harder' in theological terms, boundaries that can be drawn with more ideological confidence than the word 'imagination' suggests. To these anxieties, Hooker's reply would probably be to invite us to draw out the implications of believing that Christian community is supernatural. It is not an intensification of 'normal' human togetherness, nor is it a 'civil religion' imposed primarily by political ordinance; it is a commonalty constituted in a style of worship that is more than cerebral, that is dialogical rather than a simple process of instruction. It can be both imagined and realised if we are willing to think, as he did, about the nature of Christ and the character of historical experience. He might want to say to a good deal of modern theology that its imagination had become weak because it too readily allowed the theological agenda to be set by conflicts over human power, especially the power to determine social boundaries for the Church, and not by the classical Christological formulations. He might be worth listening to if we want to preserve the Church from new forms of elitist conceptualism (right or left); but whether we want to listen to him for those reasons or not, Hooker the theologian is more vividly and immediately the parent of Hooker the controversialist than we might have thought; and the Council of Chalcedon had more to say about parish policy in the Elizabethan Church than either Cartwright or Whitgift had suspected.

THREE

RICHARD HOOKER
(1554–1600)

Philosopher, Anglican, Contemporary

O NE OF THE PREVAILING intellectual fashions of the day in theology is the drawing up of taxonomies, ways of categorising the diverse style and methods of doing theology, or of assigning various writers to different 'types';[1] and a recent example of this is Wesley Kort's essay of 1992, *Bound to Differ: The Dynamics of Theological Discourse*.[2] Kort's typology offers (not surprisingly: there is a compulsive fascination about triadic structures) three categories: theological discourses are predominantly 'prophetic', predominantly 'priestly', or predominantly 'sapiential'. This third discourse is defined by Kort as 'starting with the needs and potentials of the human world', rather than with the critical irruption of the transcendent or the mediation of divine presence in specific privileged aspects of or moments in the world. 'Sapiential' theology worries about the ways in which the other two theological discourses are liable to become privatised; and so it turns to one or more of (again) three options. It may develop a concern with the 'natural', in the widest sense – the outer or inner ecology of human awareness, cosmology or psychology or phemonenology; it may focus on 'the problems and possibilities of human societies'; or it may search for and play with metaphors and structures for imagining an all-inclusive unity and interdependence in things. We can speak of these options as 'sapiential' because in Scripture it is the Wisdom books that most clearly exemplify these concerns, for right relation with a material environment, for 'the resolution of social conflicts' and the proper handling of social tension and areas of uncertainty, and for the imaginative authority of an integrating symbol, divine Wisdom personified, rejoicing, alluring, reflecting God, guiding reasoning creatures.[3]

While I have a fair number of reservations about Kort's thesis overall, this characterisation of one particular cluster of theological styles is good and suggestive, and its usefulness for our purposes is obvious. Hooker is, it seems, so manifestly a 'sapiential' theologian, concerned with the natural, the handling of social conflict, and the sustaining of an integrative metaphor, which, in his case, is 'Law' itself, evoked, at the end of Book I of the *Laws*, in terms very close to those of the great hymns to Wisdom in the sapiential books:[4] 'her seat is the bosom of God, her voice the harmony of the world'.[5] The sudden transition here to the feminine pronoun would alert any scripturally literate reader to the parallel with the divine *Sophia* of Proverbs, Job and (most particularly) the Wisdom of Solomon; what is claimed here for 'Law' is what the Bible claims for Wisdom. And, as Book V will remind us (V.52.3–4, 56.6; cf. 55.8 on the participation of Christ's human soul in the divine governance of the universe), Christ is scripturally and traditionally identified with God's Wisdom. The coda to Book I gives notice, indirectly but firmly, that the anchorage of church discipline in the nature and the revealing action of God is no less firm in this apologetics than in the argument from scriptural revelation and authority mounted by the opponents of the Elizabethan Settlement; indeed, it is firmer and clearer, properly understood.[6] But the working out of this is a complex story, not without paradoxical elements.

The first point worth noting is that a sapiential theology works with a clear presumption about the relation of divine nature to divine will. 'The being of God is a kind of law to his working' says

Hooker early in his argument (I.2.2). He has just proposed that law, in its most general sense, is what makes possible the attaining of specific ends or purposes, since a world in which no regularity could be depended upon would be a world in which the very idea of an 'end' would make no sense, since we could give no content to categories of cause and effect, or process and outcome. When such categories operate, the idea of law is what is presupposed – a principle of connection between events, and therefore (very importantly for later stages in the discussion) a principle of *limitation*: not every possibility can be actualised in a world where we think in terms of purposive process ('unto every end every operation will not serve' [I.2.1]). If we want to talk of God acting so as to bring about some end, we have to suppose that the divine activity too is 'law-like'; and, since God cannot be limited or conditioned by any other agency, it is what God is that determines (limits) how God acts. At I.2.5 and 6, Hooker underlines the point: it will not do to say that God's will has no cause but itself: we require a principle of consistency in speaking of God's activity, even if, from our point of view, a full *account* of what makes God's action consistent is not available. To say that this diminishes the divine freedom is to misunderstand the issue: God freely consents to the limits set to divine action by divine nature.

Hooker is at his most Thomist here, carefully closing up the gap opened up in late medieval thought between the 'absolute' power of God and the arbitrarily determined ways in which such power is concretely exercised in the universe (God *promises* to act in such and such a way, but to do so is a groundless decision, an act of unconstrained liberty). The point at issue is a highly significant one. In the Dublin Fragments[7] Hooker shows his anxiety over a doctrine of absolute divine decrees divorced from a theology of the 'natural' will of God 'to exercise his goodnes of his owne nature, by producing effects wherein the riches of the glorie thereof may appeare' (section 27); and the sermons more than once reflect the pastoral implications of a debate over the primacy of absolute divine will. But the point could be broadened: groundless divine decrees may be obeyed or implemented, but they do not lead towards a 'hinterland' of divine nature to be contemplated or enjoyed. Groundless divine will does not propose to us anything of the elusive richness of God's life as such, to be regarded with eagerness or expectation of further fulfillment: the only 'mystery' is the sheerly negative awareness of the void from which divine enactment freely comes. And because it is *necessarily* a void, it is not an object of contemplation. Yet, for Hooker, human happiness lies in 'every power and facultie of our mindes' having God as object (*Laws* I.11.2–3; cf. 11.6): conformity to law never closes on itself but disposes us for this state. And, since God as object is inexhaustible, the grounding of divine will in divine nature reinforces the awareness of the provisionality or inadequacy of what we say and do in respect of God: 'Although to know [God] be life, and joy to make mention of his name yet our soundest knowledge is to know that we know him not as indeed he is, neither can know him: and our safest eloquence concerning him is our silence' (I.2.2).

Hooker's sapiential idiom, like all theologies with a strong contemplative content, especially those in the Augustinian tradition, entails both a positive and a modest valuation of the human: positive in that (I.11.3) we alone in creation have as our goal the enjoyment of 'beauty in itself', the good *as such*, not simply the goal of an equilibrium with our circumstances which is simply good *for us*; modest in that there is an unbridgeable gap between our finite capacity and the object that satisfies us. Human perfection is thus something *progressively* realised (and always to be realised), and it cannot adequately be summed up in terms of obedience to divine commands. Our reasoning about God's nature as displayed in God's action as creator and redeemer guides our will toward those acts or policies that will intensify our vision of the divine wisdom. Part of what sets Hooker rather at an angle to much of the debate of his day is the fact that he is less interested in how God is to be 'pleased' or 'satisfied' than in how human creatures are to be healed of what impedes their vision and their joy. Forensic justification will not do for him because it can of itself give no useful account of spiritual growth; his sermon on faith in the elect insists[8] on faith as, in effect, a virtue which does not come to fullness any more rapidly than any other aspect of our 'righteousness'. And this classical concept of faith as a virtue or habit instantly puts him at odds with the mainstream of Reformed thinking.

A theology resting on law, in Hooker's sense, thus presupposes a *content* to the divine life; and this in turn implies that neither in God nor in ourselves is the bare act of self-determination intelligible or interesting (though Hooker has plenty to say about self-determination in his own way as we shall see). God's voluntary actions are all, fundamentally, aspects of the diffusion and sharing of divine life, and our proper response is receptivity to this, discernment of that divine self-bestowal and enjoyment of it. Because this is not an episodic or determinate activity, the assumption is that human existence is – as for Augustine – inescapably temporal: we are best defined as learning beings. The connections are not wholly explicit in Hooker, but there is a line to be drawn from here to the pragmatic or probabilistic, historically alert accounts of human knowing characteristic of later Anglican philosophy, from Butler to Newman (if I may be allowed, mischievously, to count Newman as an Anglican for philosophical purposes). The contingency of human learning, its dependence on (variegated) authority, the presence of a carefully modulated element of voluntarism within the whole scheme (since knowing cannot be understood without grasping that *interest* and affect are always at work in knowing subjects) – all this represents a trajectory out of Hooker, a philosophical as well as theological style that might in the contemporary philosophical climate find affinities with those who have emphasised that knowing is ineradicably a matter of contingent, conversational, perspectival and narrative development. I think here of Cavell or Nussbaum[9] on the one hand, and equally of those philosophers of science or politics, like Mary Hesse[10] for the former and Roy Bhaskar[11] for the latter, who have attempted to do justice to this dimension of contingency and historicity without falling into the trap of pure constructivism. Bhaskar's comment on Gramsci[12] admirably sums up the central concern here: 'The historicity of our knowledge . . . does not refute, but actually depends upon, the idea of the otherness of its objects (and their historicity).'

Obviously Hooker – and the whole sapiential tradition – would want to say more about the knowledge of God here, so as to avoid any misunderstanding about God being an historical object. But the force of Bhaskar's comment would have to be granted. If God's reality is *not* encountered simply as will and command, it is encountered in the law of things, in the interweaving of regularities that sustains a contingent world in intelligibility; our encounter with the nature of God as law or wisdom cannot be separated from the interpretation of this. There are, then, wide areas in which our knowledge is in fact corrigible and necessarily flexible, even when it purports to be, effectively, knowledge of a non-historical reality. If the objects of our knowing really are *other*, the idea of a finished identity between our conception and their reality is problematic, not least because these objects are themselves changing and readjusting in the continuing process that is their being-what-they-are. Thus, to know God, it seems, involves elements of flexibility and corrigibility, not because of a trivial relativist view that what's true of God changes according to circumstances, but because of the *opposite* conviction, that God remains God, a 'law unto himself', and, for precisely that reason, can only be discerned in the 'following' of the divine action within the mutable world, in a process of learning, not a moment of transparent vision or of simple submission to a decree.

This is not to say that all purported knowledge is radically under question all the time. When Hooker, in *Laws* I.15 in particular, discusses the mutability of laws, the complexity and (some would say) inconclusiveness or even incoherence of his treatment reflects very accurately the difficulty of treading a path between programmatic scepticism and a sort of historically illiterate positivism. God remains God; and therefore what constitutes human beings the *kind* of beings they are (mortality, freedom, reasoning capacity and so on) doesn't change. In more contemporary philosophical terms, we operate with readily accessible and epistemologically generous criteria as to what will count as *human* action or utterance, so that we do not waste time trying to 'decide' whether a materially recognisable human in an unfamiliar time or place can be treated, heard, or engaged with as a human thinker/speaker. Scepticism about other minds raises a nest of epistemological issues that risk distracting us from the more serious and manageable matters of philosophy. Thus there are, for Hooker, some things that simply hold for human beings as such, once you have granted the kind of universe that the ideas of law or wisdom entail; and if this is so, they hold for human society, including the society we call the Church. 'Laws natural do always bind' (I.15.1): that is to say that some of what we know is a matter of basic and non-negotiable procedure for being human before the creator, and, in Hooker's thought, such a procedure is accessible in principle for our reason functioning as it should. However, given our corrupt condition, the realising of our human happiness now depends on God's self-communication in history as well as nature – i.e. in revelation. For us *now*, concrete and historical subjects, not intellects in the abstract, the path to human happiness lies in following the law revealed in Christ, the supernatural law of faith, hope and love, which, by associating us with the eternal life of the second person of the Trinity (a theme superbly set out in the long Christological meditation of V.51–56) assures the eternal continuance of our contemplative bliss, an eternal reward which is supernatural in the sense that it is pure gift, an addition by God to the natural happiness of our fulfilment within the limits of this mortal life (I.11.5–6). Thus, although the law of faith, hope and love is not something reason can work out for itself, it has the same non-negotiable character as the basic structures of being human and being-human-in-society that we can (more or less) grasp by reason. In Hooker's terms, the law of supernatural charity is 'positive'

[46]

rather than natural, but nonetheless fixed and eternal for that (I.15.3).

To know how to be human, in short, requires us to take very seriously the fact that we are historical beings, shaped by our past: a fact that, for a classical Christian mind, has two closely related but very different sets of implications. First, we must recognise that we are never in a state of pure rationality,[13] and therefore never able, out of our own resources, successfully to negotiate the business of being properly human. Yet we learn from historical trial and error how to limit the damage of inhuman self-regard; and here is the foundation of political society (I.10.2–4). The most basic needs of humans for welfare and survival impose a kind of oblique discovery of nature's laws, and of the consequent need for government, even though nature does not specify what kind (I.10.5–6). As far as the laws of human society go, history in some degree returns us to nature's imperatives. But the same holds true of that completest and most comprehensive political society, the Church. The history that God directs, by becoming in Jesus Christ an historical agent and by moulding the Scriptures in which the law of Christ is set forth, likewise returns us to nature, to that life in which we may actualise what we are capable of and arrive at our natural end, gratuitously and supernaturally augmented with an eternal reward. We are bound to the history of Christ and to the scriptural record as our way to become what God has created us to be, lovers of the eternal beauty of God in God's self. In contrast to the contingent and imperfect learning of political trial and error, this knowledge involves us in mystical union with Christ whereby we share the eternal relation of the Word to the Father.[14] Thus the eternal, the non-negotiable constraint put upon us by Christ and Scripture has to do with how we are made contemplative saints, participants in Christ's everlasting filiation. This – and this *alone* – is for Hooker the sense in which the givenness of revelation has the same force as the law of nature.

For the second set of implications insists that we ask of our specific institutions and conventions *what end they serve*: laws are changeable when 'made for men or societies or Churches, in regard of their being such as they do not always continue' (I.15.3; 1:132.6–8). This is, of course, the subject matter of Book III, where the distinction between the means and the end of positive law (other than the basic and unchanging law of the new covenant) is carefully spelled out.[15] Once we understand what a law is *for*, we can understand whether and how it is mutable. In cases where the purpose of a divine positive law is obscure, we need a further positive mandate to abrogate it (III.10.1): though Hooker is not wholly consistent here, in that he assumes a *general* abrogation of Jewish ceremonial and dietary law after Christ, even though the precise purpose of this or that bit of the law in respect of Christ as its fulfilling and terminating end is still hidden. The reader may reasonably suspect that Hooker is extremely uneasy with the idea that the positive law of the new covenant includes specific mandates, as opposed to the fundamental doctrinal 'law' of faith in Christ and consequent hope and charity,[16] and the particular ordinances of the dominical sacraments (III.11.13). But understanding what a law is for means having some grasp of how historically limited cultures work: of *why* such and such a law is thought to produce a particular effect in these circumstances, or why what once produced that effect no longer does so (III.10.4–5). To hold on to a specific convention when it no longer effects what it did, even if the convention is held to be a positive divine mandate, is not obedience at all: and to change what we do in such circumstances is not altering God's commands but obeying the imperative contained implicitly in the failure of the mandate now to deliver what it formerly did. 'Men do not presume to change God's ordinance, but they yield thereunto requiring itself to be changed'[17] – both an ingenious and a strong formulation of a delicate point.

We can begin to see now how Hooker can sustain his claim that his system is more, not less, firmly grounded in revelation than that of his disciplinarian opponents. The assumption that Scripture is a book of positive divine law in which we find specific directives for the Church's ordering requires us to ignore the whole question of the coherence of human nature and its goals, and the coherence of God's own being. God has a 'character'; God is not pure groundless will. Therefore creation (including us) has a character: but because created nature realises its goals in contingent and temporal process, being faithful to that character and so to God's law, and so to God's being, God's self, involves being wary of any kind of positivism about laws enacted or even revealed in history, since to be bound to a set of historical positive enactments may lead us to be *unfaithful* to the real law of God, the wisdom in which we are created, when those enactments no longer effect a path to wisdom. To act in obedience to wisdom is a matter of knowing how and when to innovate:

> The Church being a body which dieth not hath always power, as occasion requireth, no less to ordain that which never was, then to ratify what hath been before. To prescribe the order of doing in all things, is a peculiar prerogative which *wisdom* hath, as Queen or Sovereign commandress over other virtues. (V.8.1)

Thus the argument is rounded off: true conformity to unchanging divine wisdom (and, it should be added, to the doctrinal formulations that embody for us how that wisdom acts and how it makes its general claim upon us) requires a flexibility in discipline and polity that is impossible for the positivist and the primitivist.

Now the modern theological reader will no doubt admire the skill and the visionary comprehensiveness of the argument; but I suspect s/he will have some awkward questions to ask. In the remainder of this chapter, I want to look at two issues in particular as they arise from this argument, and to ask whether Hooker has anything like the resource for meeting such difficulties that might commend him to a contemporary audience. Both issues are really to do with the undoubtedly odd fact that Hooker uses what is in some ways a potentially radical apologetic in defence of a conservative and perhaps authoritarian position. The first is this: granted the Church's power to make new ordinances of discipline, how in fact do we know when to make such changes? The disciplinarian is, in a way, too easy a target for Hooker: how would he meet the argument that the *de facto* order of the English church, monarch and bishops as the definitive form of government, requires just the sort of adjustment in changed circumstances that he justifies against his opponents where the introduction of episcopacy is concerned? The second question is one of obvious modern import. Language just as much as other kinds of practice is judged on its aptness to circumstances: if discipline is mutable, why not doctrine?

The first difficulty is, of course, the underlying agenda of the last four books of the *Laws*. Having given substantial hostages to fortune, Hooker has to argue, point by point or case by case, the 'negative' brief that, in all matters where disciplinarians express unease, there is no conclusive case for any change beyond what the Settlement itself recognises. This is no less a *tour de force* than the earlier argument, though it has a far more ambivalent sound to the modern ear. It depends quite heavily on assuming that Church and State have an executive authority with a reasonable presumption in its favour; and, as the argument of these four books develops, that 'reasonable presumption' slips closer and closer towards the sanction of divine positive law, though without ever *quite* getting there, in either the ecclesiastical or the wider political realm. What stops it quite getting there is the fact that Hooker holds on to his opposition to the idea that any given political discipline, including monarchy and episcopacy, derives normally from *unmediated* divine mandate: granting this possibility would have unravelled most of his earlier case. What we must envisage – and it is spelled out in an uncomfortably compressed way in VIII.2.5–7 – is a kind of primordial self-determination by political communities seeking to follow the law of nature by finding for themselves organs of executive power. Book VII never directly claims that episcopacy is instituted by Christ: but the apostolic power is the source of the episcopal, and the episcopal, and the episcopal represents a localising and channelling of the more primitive power,[18] universally accepted and endorsed by the first churches. Likewise, in Book VIII, monarchy in general is not the result of divine appointment (we have already been told, remember, at 1.10.5, that 'Nature tieth not to any one' form of rule); yet, once decided upon and accepted, it has a sanction beyond that of the community's consent at any one moment, a 'divine right'.

Throughout the *Laws*, Hooker assumes that communities of reasoning beings have the right to determine the shape of their political life; and indeed, because of our fallen state, they have a *duty* to find an effective form of executive power for the restraint of vice. We might have been capable in the Garden of Eden of living without executive government, but our present fallibility, idleness of mind, and corruption of habit, visible to the wisest among us, require a potentially coercive power.[19] Hooker, like the good Augustinian he is (and the good patriarchalist he consequently is), has no particular optimism about the moral discernment of the mass of human beings, for all that he greatly privileges the self-determining right of any human community. Now, if these primordial self-determinations are truly for the sake of God's eternal law and our contemplative happiness, we might better understand them if perhaps we go back to some of the general observations at the very beginning of the *Laws*. Law in a plural and contingent world is precisely the self-limitation of divine power so that specific and interdependent processes may go forward in regular fashion: if the goals are diverse, though coherent, God's power logically cannot be present in each substance or process as an *infinite* potentiality. Only God as God possesses infinite liberty – and even that is not a liberty of utterly arbitrary self-definition, since God is by nature thus-and-not-otherwise. So we could say that the characteristic shape of law is self-limitation. The community seeking to conserve its conformity to the law of God cannot, in the world of fallen history, remain for ever in a state of political innocence; it must decide how to enact its aims, and so must give up its indeterminate potential.

Prompted by any number of varied considerations, about the specific problems it faces, the local difficulties or deficiencies it wants to remedy, it commits itself to this or that executive polity. *Once that commitment has been made*, observing its consequences becomes a matter of obedience to divine law, even when there is full awareness of the contingency, in a certain sense, of this polity in its origins, and the mutability of its detail in a possible future. It acquires this sanction because *this* is the way the community has chosen to establish its identity in a world where limited identities (natural, personal and political) are constantly in precarious balance. To pretend that this constructed identity is suddenly (and I think the operative word is 'suddenly') a disposable fiction is not only to be blind to one's own conditioning by that social history, but to ignore the ways in which *this* historical identity has become part of a wider network, has entered into the self-definition of other communities – which is to ignore that 'sociable', mutual dimension of the law-governed world that Hooker touches on in Book I (3.5, 8.6, 9.1) and in his sermon on pride, where he memorably defines justice as 'the virtue whereby that good which wanteth in ourselves we receive inoffensively at the hands of others' (Sermon III; Keble, vol. III, p. 618).

There is a certain *prima facie* conservative implication here, which Hooker manifestly exploits; and the emphasis on the sanction that the enforcement of such positive law possesses reminds us unambiguously that part of the polemical purpose of the *Laws* was to secure a rationale for legal action against religious dissidents. Yet the discussion does not take the final step into that absolute positivism of sovereignty that has been such an incubus upon English legal theory up to the present,[20] and Hooker is not the most comfortable of bedfellows for a purely authoritarian, un-compromisingly divine-right model of secular or ecclesiastical government. The contemporary student would probably want to say that the community's self-limitation remains rather more func-tional than Hooker is entirely happy to grant – just as (for us) in the natural order, the reimaginings and readjustments of the evolutionary process militate against the idea of a *single* primordial limitation of possibilities in fixed species, so in politics the constant question of the accountability of polity to the human ends it serves cannot be evaded. The primordial self-determining community is not now simply an etiological myth, forever separated from us by a single act of self-denuding decision. If human subjects retain the rational – and therefore risktaking – liberties with which Hooker's anthropology endows them, and if wisdom in the cosmos is itself 'revisionary', the compelling obviousness of a once-for-all delegation of power is a good deal lessened.

But what Hooker's thesis also reminds us of in a contemporary context is the perennial seductiveness of a radical programme un-interested in what has made us the subjects we now are. Changing polities is a futile exercise if we are not prepared to come to terms with the history that conditions and limits us, that gives us the very language in which to pose political questions. Ignore this, and you end up with the modern version of primitivist positivism (we can both discover and return to an age before the distortions of dualist/partiarchal/exploitative consciousness) or timeless rationalism (the principles of liberal secularist democracy are *obvious*, and the dissenter – the Muslim, for instance – is not really a partner in reasonable conversation). Hooker at least obliges us to think about how we came to pose our questions like this, and how, therefore, our questions and aspirations are continuous with those of our history. To ask, for instance, why monarchy ever looked like a compelling model of how to direct human beings to a goal of happiness may be of more political use than a bald dismissal of it. If we are able to 'talk' with our history, assuming some common human ground about ultimate goods being sought, we should be able to see how history is both *ourselves* and *other* – rather this than that attitude which, by assuming the obvious reasonableness of where we are now and how we talk now, simply sees history as an unsuccessful approximation to the triumphant 'sameness' of modernity (and so also sees the non-standardly modern aspects of the present world as primitive or retarded).

Hooker does at least insist that what we are is *made*, that we cannot reconstruct 'original positions', and that whatever political futures we desire have to be reworkings of what historical limitation has constructed for us, even if – as we hope – they can be more than repetitions.

What, then, of the second set of questions, about doctrinal formulations? Part of the answer has been given in what has already been said. *A fortiori*, we cannot pretend that we are theological innocents, timelessly confronting the mystery of God's action.[21] We are not here talking about a voluntary self-limitation, but about a call or imperative or transforming gift that 'limits' us, whether we choose or no. There can be no beginning all over again here – the determinations have, in some sense, been made *for* us, first of all in creation, in our being the sort of beings we are, and then in a redemption whose point is to free us to be such beings. It is not up to us to 'choose' our final ends, because we do not choose our nature. In this case, then, even more than with matters of polity, how we act and talk is conditioned by a history – not a history, this time, of our decisions and their consequences, but a history of attempts to bring to speech *that which* determines us. Doctrine, in other words, is always a catching up with something prior to us: we do not (in both the technical and the colloquial senses of the words) 'have priority' when we try to speak doctrinally. When we reckon with the ways in which doctrinal history, like political history, conditions the questions we ask and how we ask them, the essential difference, in Hooker's perspective, between the two kinds of conditioning is that political history is about *means* to the *ends* that doctrinal language specifies. If we treat our doctrinal language as revisable in the same sense as our talk about polity, we risk treating our human ends as negotiable, as potentially under human control or at the mercy of human circumstance; and this fragments the whole underlying sapiential model, depending as this model does on our final determination by the nature of God as the object we find our bliss in contemplating, the life we are fulfilled in sharing.

Hooker's proscription of doctrinal revision, then, has a clear logic to it. We may have more problems than he did about the historical conceptualities of doctrinal statement, we may well want to say that doctrinal utterance *does* involve human choices, human self-determinations, unless we believe that revelation comes in well-formed statements to start with. But the question Hooker poses for the doctrinal revisionist is a serious one, one that needs articulation in our contemporary theological debates. Doctrine is about our end (and our beginning); about what in our humanity is not negotiable, dispensable, vulnerable to revision according to political convenience or cultural chance and fashion. Deny this, and you must say that humanity or the human good is, in some significant way, within our power to determine: which may sound emancipatory for a few minutes, until you remember that, in a violent and oppressive world, it is neither good news nor good sense to propose that definitions of the human lie in human hands, when those hands are by no means guaranteed to be the instruments of a mind formed by contemplative reason – or even what passes for reason in the liberal and universalist ethos of 'our' democracies. Doctrine purports to tell us what we are for, and what the shape is of a life lived in accordance with the way things are, and how such a life becomes accessible to us, even in the middle of the corruptions and unfreedom of a shadowed history. Hooker's general apologetic for revealed religion would need a fair amount of reworking in our more ironic age, but his challenge is still worth listening to. If we are not somehow bound by what God is and what we are, however stumblingly and inadequately we can speak of these things, what possibility is there of sustaining a belief in the common good of human creatures beyond the terms of a minimalist discourse about survival?

Hooker – like the Anglican tradition as a whole, it is tempting to add – is tantalisingly hard to pigeonhole. I have been trying to show that his schemas refuse to be classified once and for all as simply 'conservative' or 'radical', and that aspects of what is undeniably a local polemic, very much of its time and place, set off chains of reflection with an uncomfortable contemporary edge. But the final comment I'd want to make is to underline the significance of a 'sapiential' theology in an age when the theological debate so readily polarises between one or another variety of positivism (biblically fundamentalist, ecclesiastically authoritarian, or whatever) and a liberalism without critical or self-critical edge. It is not a matter of interest only to theologians either: as I have hinted, the development of a proper political anthropology requires something of the balance that a sapiential scheme offers between objectivism (the otherness of what we know) and a recognition of responsive creativity in persons (the inevitability of self-determining decisions). If this is part of Hooker's legacy, part too of a distinctively Anglican legacy of 'contemplative pragmatism' against the background of basic creedal and liturgical commitments, it is something worth celebrating and worth developing – in what often looks like the onset of a very *un*sapiential era in secular and ecclesial politics.

FOUR

GEORGE HERBERT

(1593–1633)

Inside Herbert's *Afflictions*

I read, and sigh, and wish I were a tree:
For sure then I should grow
To fruit or shade: at least some bird would trust
Her household to me, and I should be just.

THE FIRST OF Herbert's five *Affliction* poems is, from one point of view, the least complex: it simply evokes sterility. The poem resolutely refuses to move, qualifying every apparent emotional or spiritual shift with a rhetorical step (or two) backwards. God has lured the poet into commitment: Herbert's 'heart' is given, as the very first line tells us, and his freedom is apparently mortgaged. Now, with the bleak history of loss, sickness and frustrated hopes behind, he is paralysed. There is enough 'Academick praise' of (presumably) his professional rhetoric at Cambridge to contain his anger at the failure of his secular ambitions; and this gradually leads 'where I could not go away nor persevere', to ordination. 'Now I am here' there is no clarity about the value or worth of the life: God has provided a 'crosse-bias', slanting Herbert's career from its (apparently) natural course, yet making nothing visibly fruitful of his new calling. He reads and sighs, wishing to be 'just', that is, 'justified' – a bold appropriation of theological resonances, just like 'persevere' a few lines earlier.

Here is one way into the inside of this poem, whose difficulty is its very refusal of difficulty, its refusal to articulate any coherent movement in its rhetoric right up to the last few lines. And to go a little further inside the poem takes us into an area that is in fact of central importance for Herbert's rhetoric overall (an area charted more dramatically in *Dialogue*, to which I'll be returning later). 'Perseverance' and 'justification' are not only theological technicalities, but technicalities of great contemporary moment for Herbert. Perseverance is the gift that manifests predestination to eternal life in Reformed theology, and it is intimately connected with that assurance of salvation that was so fiercely debated between orthodox Calvinists and others in the seventeenth-century Church of England; justice and justification are not only the key concepts of the entire Reformation era, but are central to the controversies in which Hooker was involved in the closing decades of the sixteenth century, controversies that helped to set the agenda for the Church of Herbert's day. And what Herbert does here – as he does (though less dramatically) for the word 'predestination' in *The Thanksgiving* – is to drop these terms almost casually, it seems, into a quite untechnical context, with the result that their theological sense is 'made strange'. The theologian has to think again here, where the terms adopted for technical use are bedded in ordinary colloquialism.

Herbert cannot persevere. Of course he can't, the Calvinist might say: perseverance is a matter of pure grace, being held by God's predestinating will. But isn't that actually what Herbert is saying? He is unable to desert God, and that ought to be a sign of assurance. Only it does not 'assure' in the usual sense, but intensifies frustration; what is the strict Calvinist to make of this? Has the gift been given or not? Herbert subverts the scheme in which the question can be asked, partly by intimating that 'perseverance' is an empty word if you have no sense or conception of a task to be persevered in: nothing will tell him what God now wants of him, and there are no external marks of fruitfulness such as would confirm the assurance of an orthodox Reformed believer. There is no 'biography' of faith to be written, only the 'Now I am here' of motionless frustration and doubt; no unfolding of a perseverance marked by the gradual appearance of good effects. As an excellent contemporary critic of Herbert observes, he is pervasively suspicious of charting any *process* of growth.[1] The effect is to put perseverance as a theological motif in a very odd light: what can it mean but the impossibility of falling out of God's hands? But how is that impossibility experienced (even when acknowledged) except as an immobilising, even imprisoning dependence, where there are no tokens of assurance in the movement of a life towards fruitfulness? But perseverance is a word that carries overtones of the will to carry something to completion, and sits uncomfortably with Herbert's picture of the bare duration of his own immobility.

We are left in the awkward position of being able to draw no theological conclusion about 'perseverance' from Herbert's experience: the theology of perseverance as a gift does not answer the question of whether his state, 'Now I am here', is or is not a state of grace. And exactly the same problem is evoked by his use of 'just' a little later on. The sterility of his present condition means that he is not 'just' – an odd use to modern ears, though we still speak of 'justifying our existence'. Herbert's use here, however, as in the first stanza of *Easter* ('His life may make thee gold, and much more, just') is illuminated by a discussion such as we find in Hooker's Sermon III ('Of the Nature of Pride'): here 'the nature of justice in general' is defined in terms of the interdependence of creation, and the 'matter for exercise of justice' in such goods as may be communicated from one to another. 'Justice is the virtue whereby that good which wanteth in ourselves we receive inoffensively at the hands of others.'[2] The likelihood of Herbert's having known this text is not very high, since the greater part of it remained unpublished until the nineteenth century; but it puts with great clarity the implication of the doctrine laid down early in Book I of Hooker's *Laws* (I.3.5), that law or right, *jus*, applied to things not only in respect of their inherent and distinct structures, but 'as they are sociable parts united into one body; a law which bindeth them each to serve unto other's good'.[3] Behind this, of course, stands Augustine (especially the 19th book of the *City of God*) and St Thomas' account of *justitia* in, for example, S.Th.II.IIae, 57.I.c: 'what we call "just" in our actions is what responds to some other reality according to some sort of fitness (*aequalitas*)'. In other words, being 'just' in the terms of the classical Christian moral and metaphysical scheme with which Herbert was familiar had to do with the kind of relationship with other things in the universe in which their needs are appropriately met by the subject's activity. What does 'justice' mean if divorced from this?

Yet such a divorce is what a strict Reformed theology seems to require. To become 'just' (to be justified) is to acquire a status, not a role; it is to be regarded by God in a certain way – i.e. it is a 'passive' matter as far as we are concerned. Second- and third-generation Calvinists had sharpened the distinction between the grace that makes us 'just', gives us the status of righteous or acceptable beings in God's eyes, and the grace that makes us holy, actively living out our condition. Herbert invokes, in the margin, as it were, a classical Catholic sense of 'justice', and declares its absence in his experience; the Reformed sense of the word is thus presented as a matter not to be experienced – like perseverance in fact. Experientially, Herbert is not 'just'; yet he is in God's hands, taken away by grace from his own 'wayes', and what is justification but this?

The effect of these unobtrusively contentious words in the poem is to impress on the reader – Herbert's theologically alert reader – how controversial theological idiom may be, how theology can wrench a word out of its territory and apparently evacuate its meaning; and this appears as specially true of aspects of the Reformed divinity that Herbert himself took for granted (it is always worth remembering that Herbert was not a Laudian). What is he at? He is not covertly polemicising against Calvinism as such, in the name of a more integral or Catholic theology. Hooker's magnificent harmonising of active and passive 'justice' in his famously controversial sermon on justification in 1586[4] is a long way from Herbert's concern. The tension of the poem arises precisely from his acceptance of a strongly Calvinist sense of 'perseverance' and 'justice', a sense that is sharply at odds with traditional or habitual usage; with 'perseverance', he even goes rather further, pressing on the Calvinist linkage of perseverance with assurance as if to ask whether this link really makes sense. But in both cases, the overall issue is a subtly indicated schism between theology and certain sorts of experience: what 'perseverance' and 'justice' mean for the Reformed believer cannot be spelled out in the description of states of mind or habits of life.

The search for such experiential illumination is rapidly and dramatically brought to a head in the poem's difficult final stanza – the point at which the unspoken difficulty of the whole poem is allowed to surface. We should take 'I must be meek' and 'must be stout' as ironic: this is the voice of orthodox wisdom, the 'I must' meaning (as often in the literature of the period), 'I am told I ought to'. The counsel ironically cited is, in this case, not so much that of a Reformed theology, but rather that of the pastorally moderate critics of Calvinist rigorism on the subject of assurance. To turn again to Hooker: his sermon on 'The Certainty and Perpetuity of Faith', preached in 1585 or 1586 (Sermon I, first published in 1612 and reissued, along with others, in 1622[5]), presents a severe and thoroughgoing critique of the idea that assurance is exclusive of doubt or depression, or even the conviction of unfruitfulness; it reads at times almost like a pastoral gloss on many of Herbert's poems, and Herbert's knowledge of this text is overwhelmingly probable. Hooker's description of the state of mind of the person without tangible or experiential assurance is worth quoting at length:

[We become convinced] that we are clean crost out of God's

book, that he regards us not, that he looketh upon others, but passeth by us like a stranger to whom we are not known. Then we think, looking upon others, and comparing them with ourselves, Their tables are furnished day by day; earth and ashes are our bread: they sing to the lute, and they see their children dance before them; our hearts are heavy in our bodies as lead, our sighs beat as thick as a swift pulse, our tears do wash the beds wherein we lie: the sun shineth fair upon their foreheads; we are hanged up like bottles in the smoke, cast into corners like the shards of a broken pot: tell us not of the promises of God's favour, tell such as do reap the fruit of them; they belong not to us, they are made to others.[6]

Hooker's response throughout the sermon (one of his most concise and rhetorically powerful) is to point out that a 'perfect', fully conscious faith might delude us into thinking that faith *as a human virtue* saved us. Our faith can be no more perfect than our righteousness, in itself; or else,

What need we the righteousness of Christ? His garment is superfluous: we may be honourably clothed with our own robes, if it be thus. But let them beware who challenge to themselves a strength which they have not, lest they lose the confortable support of that weakness which indeed they have.[7]

We must, then, learn to be 'fruitful in weakness though weak in faith' – a paradox very close to Herbert's, as is the account of the godly as those whose 'faith, when it is at the strongest, is but weak; yet even then when it is at the weakest, so strong, that utterly it never faileth'.[8] Hooker is addressing himself directly to those who, 'by extremity of grief', 'find not themselves in themselves': they cannot find what is actually within them, and 'lament as for a thing which is past finding . . . as if that were not which indeed is, and as if that which is not were; as if they did not believe when they do, and as if they did despair when they do not'.[9]

I have quoted at length from this sermon because of its bearing on Herbert's rhetoric here and elsewhere; as I have said, it reads like a response to Herbert's anguish, and is, indeed, one of the most imaginative and sensitive pastoral texts on this subject in the whole English Protestant tradition. But we should not miss the irony or anger in Herbert's final stanza. Hooker's impeccably sound counsel produces the quite unexpectedly abrupt reaction, 'Well, I will change the service, and go seek/Some other master out.' The problem (as Hooker[10] in fact foresees in his sermon: 'Tell this to a man that hath a mind deceived by too hard an opinion of himself and it doth but augment his grief') is that the counsel itself cannot touch the desire for experiential assurance. The poem so far has presented us with the image of a faith, a perseverance and a righteousness that do not touch the poet's sense of self: the initial sweetness of a felt enjoyment of God's grace has disappeared, and no fruitful virtues have been born. Alienated from 'natural' fulfilment, there seems no 'supernatural' fulfilment to supplant it; what reason, then, can there be for fidelity to a 'service' that has no inner or outer effect? Patience in weakness is no answer. And the closing couplet of the poem, notoriously a puzzle for interpreters, both articulates the despair and near-blasphemy to which the whole poem has been working, and encodes a kind of resolution.

> Ah my deare God! Though I am clean forgot,
> Let me not love thee, if I love thee not.

'Though I am clean forgot' looks at first like an invitation to God to withdraw his saving grace. Better to be reprobate than unable to love when God invites or permits or enables me to love. If God will not make good his gift, it is better that the gift be withdrawn. Surely, the couplet asks, my salvation is my business: why can there not be an 'I' that is aware of itself as actively loving? God's enablement of love by his election never connects with the experience of a loving agent: so what is the point of the enabling gift?

But this primary and harsh reading is perhaps shadowed by a different one, which reverses the sentiment: God forbid that I should see myself as a lover of God if I do not actually love God – although such love involves my forgetting myself. Even if no perceptible transformation in my sense of self occurs, even if the claims of the conscious ego are to be forgotten, better that than that God indulge me by 'letting' me experience a love which falls short of what God's gift actually demands in God's own terms.

If this double reading is right, the conclusion of this poem is both protest and answer. There are several instances in Herbert's work (*The Collar* being the best known) where the poet's protest is silenced directly by God's voice: here the concluding ejaculation, the prayer simultaneously for the gift of false and of true love, carries the frustration of the whole poem and answers it by carrying also the gift of an authentic prayer. Perseverance and assurance are uncovered by the bare possibility of an abiding desire not to be deceived or satisfied with anything less than God; and if we were to turn to the poems entitled *Perseverance* and *Assurance*, we should see this reinforced. *Perseverance* (not published with *The Temple* and surviving in the Williams manuscript)[11] sweeps aside the question of usefulness or self-approbation, leaving – as the mark of perseverance on the human side – no more than a 'Clinging and crying, crying without cease/Thou art my rock, thou art my rest'. And *Assurance* repudiates any 'hope and comfort' I might derive 'from my self' to turn to the 'self' that God gives in his covenant:

> as when the league was made
> Thou didst at once thy self indite,
> And hold my hand, while I did write.

The end of *Affliction (I)* is both a 'clinging and crying' and a 'divine' answer written by the human hand, an overwriting of the poet's expressed desire by the divine inscribing of the desire for true love, even at the cost of the self, as it has been poetically constructed. This desire for truth is not something that simple introspection can turn up – otherwise we should have nothing more than another form of experiential assurance. Poetically, it can only appear as what is left when the language of the protesting self has been allowed to exhaust itself ('what is left': we may think there of Herbert's repeated playing on the different senses of 'rest' in poems like *Perseverance*). The paradox of this poetics is that the self's urgency for a sense of conscious participation in grace can be answered and overturned only in its full exposure to the light of language. Whatever is left to be written, or whatever writes, when the self has had its say, is the word of assurance: which is why, as in *Affliction (I)*, all comfort must be refused until the ending simultaneously brings the self's rebellion to a culmination and quells it. And it may be worth observing in passing that such a conclusion is a partial Herbertian absolution of Hooker, whose final specific against despair is to appeal to an obstinate and 'secret' desire to believe as the one argument that 'the subtilty of infernal powers will never be able to dissolve'.[12] A partial absolution: for Herbert, his desire must (and can only) be articulated in the oblique and dangerous mode of a kind of 'posturing' in despair or revolt.

Does this at all answer, though, the underlying unease about the self? Is the saved soul only a passive, a virtually empty reality? This is the problem directly addressed in *Dialogue*, a brief but highly charged poem, whose 'difficulty' once again appears most plainly at the last moment. It begins with a quite deceptive lyricism (a faint reminiscence in the wording and meter of the opening, of Donne's 'Sweetest love, I do not goe . . .'); but the second half of the first stanza, with its four-times-repeated rhyme, introduces a note of something like querulous insistence, and we are warned that this dialogue will not be an exchange of lyrical pleasantries. Already there is a half-spoken threat: how much easier to subdue the temptation to infidelity if I were convinced that I were worth loving! If I am not enabled to see that, the covenant with God has no 'delight or hope', for it has nothing to do with me. Can I be grateful for a love so gratuitous that it is apparently indifferent to who and what I am? God's answer is that of *A True Hymne* and *Love (III)*: 'As when th' heart says (sighing to be approved)/ *O could I love!* and stops: God writeth, Loved.' And 'Love took my hand . . .'

In the *Dialogue*, God charges the poet with spoiling what God values, and argues further that, since God has paid the price of humankind on the cross, has been exchanged, sold, for our sake, he alone knows the value of the human soul. This, however, does not silence the poet: uniquely, for Herbert, the divine interruption doesn't settle the question, and argument continues, in a further stanza in which a certain complexity of thought begins to build up. Nothing I can do or imagine will present me to myself as an acceptable object for God's love; so my reaction to that gift can be no more than a passive acceptance of an unintelligible trans- action in which my active selfhood has no part. It cannot matter how I receive what's given. If God insists that he alone knows my value, then he alone has responsibility for the work of salvation: 'the way is none of mine'. The language of 'disclaiming' here picks up one of the possible meanings of 'waving' in the first stanza, the *waiving* of a right or claim: Herbert, in 'disclaiming' the plan of redemption, may be either protesting that he has no part in it or repudiating its effects. The rather puzzling line, 'sinne disclaims and I resigne', may be another deliberately ambiguous statement. To 'disclaim' what is offered in redemption is the work of sin, and the 'resigning' that follows is an abandonment of the hope of salvation. But also: I disclaim rights or part in the process of salvation; and sin likewise disclaims rights over me, waives its claims, so that I am left (as in *Affliction (I)* immobilised between two worlds, the realm of sin from which I have been delivered, and the realm of grace in which I can do or understand nothing.

The second divine reply seizes on the senses of 'resignation' to enforce its point. That I should 'resigne' is exactly what God wants, because such an act mirrors God's own activity. But, on

God's part, resignation is a free self-surrender, a spontaneous self-forgetting in love, which exposes God to the extreme of suffering; in particular, God resigns his 'glorie and desert', resigns all consideration of what is due to him. His act is 'without repining', without regret or reluctance; but the resignation the poet has offered is a distancing of the self from the process of redemption, on the grounds that this process bears no relation to merit or desert, and so it fails to mirror God's act. As in *Love (III)*, the point is that acceptance of the divine love simply requires the abandonment of all effort at assessing my own worth, negatively or positively. To go on being conscious of a disparity between God's grace and my deserving can be, not humility, but a refusal to let go of the self; and the complaint that grace has failed to remake me in an 'acceptable' shape reflects the same refusal. God's attitude to me ought to correlate with mine to myself: if I despise myself, God should despise me; and conversely, if God approves me, why can I not approve myself? What grace must overcome is this assumption; but it can only do so when I am no longer looking at myself.

Hence the rhetoric of the poem's conclusion. God's words relentlessly enforce attention to what God has done, the insistent rhyme here serving to press home the consistency of the divine self-abandoning; and the final line is one of Herbert's boldest moves, a silencing of God by the poet. Complaint or rebellion is not simply quelled by the divine intervention: it is converted. The poet's voice responding is precisely the voice of a resignation that goes some way towards mirroring God's, in that it appears as an irregular, spontaneous 'motion' (to use a word profoundly significant for Herbert and his age). God speaks at the end of the poem in the brokenness of the poetic voice and the resigning of the argument: and the 'heart' of the human speaker introduces itself into the rhyme of divine action. It is a particularly powerful example of how the 'unconsidered', rhetorically unrhetorical response of the poet to God (*Affliction (II)*, *The Thanksgiving*, *Jordan (I)*, *Grief*) articulates the point to which a Christian poetry must come, the abandonment of self-conscious skill in a giving-place to God: here, what gives it especial force is the presenting of this abandonment as a breaking-in on the words of God. The completing of the divine utterance is the converted human voice, even if its conversion is violently expressed.

Two overall themes emerge from the poems we have been examining. The first has to do with the character of Christian poetry, a matter of concern, as we know, to Herbert's contemporaries. Why write a poetry whose destiny (or even vocation) is to be annulled by the overriding voice of God (since a successfully edifying poetry would involve the writer in an experienced gratification that would overthrow grace)? These poems (as I've intimated) enact the movement of a grace of self-dispossession within their own words. When all's said and done, the receiving of God's grace is something like other human acts: there is a story and a language for it; and it is clear from Scripture and the saints, as it is clear from the whole of Herbert's prose and poetry, that human beings are called to show the nature and action of God in what they do and say. Thus God is glorified by rehearsing the story of conversion and seeking a language for praise. But the story must not be a distant or an abstract one: the language must show it now. How, then, can it be shown except by a poetry that licenses the extreme of protest so as to show the extreme of God's power to silence or to transfigure that protest? Herbert's Christian poetry works with a deliberate and risky 'invitation'; of extreme sensibility. No reply but God's can be admitted to quiet the merciless analysis of discontent and sterility – which is why Herbert cannot be Hooker. Herbert is no less a pastoral theologian, but his pastoral idiom is entirely self-involving, not diagnostic or therapeutic in a way external to the subject's sense of self.

This extremism should not be read as a simple self-deprecation or a less simple (pathological?) self-hatred. It is a conscious and careful 'indulging' of self-doubt (a perfectly authentic self-doubt, but nonetheless a deliberate and literary construction for that) so as to invite a presence or voice of unanswerable authority; so as to make the poetry transparent to the authority of divine action, not by blending the authorial voice with God's, but by constructing an authorial voice that can be decisively and finally negated – the voice that flirts so alarmingly in these poems with the idea of a rejection of what God has chosen, a refusal of God's decree. It is a very Calvinistic extremism, in that it dramatises the confidence of the elect in a divine choice completely unconditioned by and unaffected by the subjectivity – past, present or future – of the believer. It is a pushing at the limit of Calvinist orthodoxy: how can election be understood in such a way as to be compatible with entertaining the thought of inviting reprobation? Herbert's is very nearly a *reductio ad absurdum*: the securely elect can contemplate infidelity and radical doubt with a vertiginous freedom denied to those who seek signs of election in their own thought or action. In this sense, it is the sovereignty of grace for Herbert that makes possible the dangerous indulgence and psychological complexity of poems such as the two we are examining.

What saves this from being a sort of posturing on the brink of the abyss, the pseudo-heroism that is really a 'gesture of contempt to those who lacked the courage thus to leap' into the void (to borrow a phrase from Donald MacKinnon's reflections on Paul Tillich[13]), is a twofold quality in Herbert's verse that brings us to our second point. His deliberate extremism remains always the anatomy of a particular autobiographical sense of pain and futility, the feeling of what is essentially an undramatic agony of boredom and wasted time. Very seldom is the extremism given a 'baroque' formulation, an extremism of expression: when it is, as in *Grief*, it is normally to be cancelled and shown to be false. And so the confidence that permits this psychological extravagance can only be spoken in terms that are supremely unheroic ('Clinging and crying . . .'). The language remains, so often, bald and prosaic, and the resolutions wholly unflattering to a would-be heroic will. In these two ways, the poetry continues to insist that grace is not to be unearthed by introspection – or, rather, not unearthed directly by introspection, but only by the oblique route of looking

[69]

on my inner turmoil and rebellion so as to exhaust its possibilities for analysis, and thus evoke the silence in which what remains is, simply, God. The sense in which it is misleading just to call Herbert a Calvinist, *sans phrase*, has to do with his evident repudiation of third-generation Reformed theologies of assurance, which could so easily slip back into a search for the ground of grace in oneself. Within the controversial topography of the English Church of his day, he is neither Puritan nor Arminian – which explains how he could be read so enthusiastically by both Charles I and Richard Baxter, and by many others on opposite sides of the Civil War and the ecclesiastical controversies. What I have called the 'Calvinist' quality of his extremism and his confidence is a far more radical Calvinism than that of, say, Hooker's critics of the 1580s and 90s, a reappropriation of Calvin's own overriding concern for the location of saving power absolutely and exclusively in the liberty of God.

The paradox here is that such a radicalism brings Herbert to the same position as that of the major Catholic contemplatives of the preceding century (and of his near-contemporary, Augustine Baker). Teresa and John of the Cross were both somewhat suspect to Catholic authority for appearing to teach that it was possible to be assured of final salvation: yet both (Teresa at least in her later years) insisted on a sharp separation between the sense or experience of being in God's favour or united to God and the fact of a confirmation of the covenant between God and the soul. For them, as for Herbert, it is confidence in the willingness of God to save that permits the uninhibited expression of felt uncertainty, even the sense of reprobation. Assurance is only in the endurance of the desire for truth and for God, a desire which, because it is effectively without determinate content, remains experientially problematic (to say the least). To discover that there are no immanent grounds for confidence is the surest way of remitting responsibility to God, and so of honouring God for his sovereign freedom.

But does this mean that, for Herbert or his Catholic counterparts, God can only be honoured by a kind of dishonouring of the human? Will it do (echoing Herbert's complaint in *Dialogue*) to ground the value of the self in God's love alone, in such a way as to leave the self intrinsically unloveable? Do we want to be the objects of a purely groundless desire? Insofar as these questions still presuppose the perspective of a self-judging consciousness, there can be no real answer short of the 'resignation' to which the poetry moves. But there are hints of another and less direct response. To be – humanly speaking – the object of another's desire is both a healing and a frightening matter, because we all fear that dissolution into the needs and fantasies of another that desire can entail, and yet cannot learn self-love without the love of others. A human desire indifferent to the particular sub-jectivity of the one desired can only appear as menacing ('You say you love me, but you aren't *interested* in me at all'; Julian to Bradley in Iris Murdoch's *The Black Prince*). But the divine eros evoked in *Dialogue* and elsewhere is not another hungry ego threatening my own. It is enacted in self-dispossession, in (as *Affliction (II)* spells out) an appropriation of my own standpoint as grieving, resentful, rebellious. That God sues for my soul does not entail any de-realising of myself, furthermore, since it is the divine eros which is responsible for the existence of my particular selfhood in the first place. The soul is 'my clay, my creature'; and we may think of 'Such a strength, as makes his guest' in *The Call*, or 'who made the eyes but I?' in *Love (III)*. Creation means that God desires me to be before he desires me to be redeemed (this is, of course, to bracket out the notorious Calvinist debate over whether some souls are created in order to be reprobated; I don't think that Herbert provides any evidence as to where he might have stood on this issue, though a pure prelapsarianism would be hard to reconcile with some of what he says about creation, in *The Pulley* for instance, and about the vocation of 'man' in general, as in *The Window, Prayer, Giddinesse* or *Miserie*).

And what God desires is that the created self imitate his own eros, loving God in forgetfulness of 'desert' or status. But human resignation remains (of course) unlike God's: it must be constructed, brought to life, whereas God's is the sheer enactment of his being. Our resigning in love is the fruit, the birth, of a protracted exploring of the possibilities of not loving, refusing the gift, an exploring of the strangeness of 'love unknown' which licenses even our rebellion because it is dependent on nothing but itself. We cannot come to resignation without a history of faith and interwoven unfaith; and for us as speaking creatures, that history is to be shown in language, and the triumph of grace shown in the capture and transforming of language, in the bold and risky idioms of a poetry like Herbert's. We are not called simply to silence, but to a silence shaped by protest, a love (even a self-love) constrained out of self-despair by the ineradicable presence of God's desire. Herbert's poetry is that constraint at work.

FIVE

B.F. WESTCOTT

(1825–1901)

The Fate of Liberal Anglicanism

I N 1883, BROOKE FOSS WESTCOTT was asked by the Bishop of Peterborough to resign from the canonry he then held at Peterborough Cathedral. Westcott was pained and bewildered; no explanation was forthcoming, except for the bishop's rather unconvincing charge that Westcott had been neglecting his duties in the diocese. He had held the canonry for thirteen years along with the Regius Chair at Cambridge, but, like many of his generation in comparable positions, spent a large proportion of his vacations at work in cathedral and diocese; he was able to demonstrate without difficulty that his conscientiousness in diocesan duties had not suffered from his academic commitments.[1] It is hard not to conclude that Bishop Magee was anxious about Westcott's reputation. The Revised Version of the Bible had appeared two years earlier, arousing much controversy, and Westcott's name was closely allied to this ill-starred project. Sixteen years earlier, a pamphlet of Westcott's had been turned down for publication by SPCK as doctrinally unsound,[2] and a faint air of danger had hung around his name. Magee was solidly conservative in his ecclesiastical loyalties (he was one of those who objected to Frederick Temple's consecration as Bishop of Exeter in 1869, on the grounds of Temple's association with *Essays and Reviews*[3]); he may have felt that, at a time when the Revised Version was attracting a good deal of criticism in Convocation and elsewhere, he needed to signal some distance between himself and one of the leading spirits in the revision – even though he had offered Westcott the canonry, together with the post of examining chaplain, at a time when Westcott was already regarded with some suspicion in the strictest circles.

Whatever the reasons, Westcott complied (and was almost immediately nominated by Gladstone to a stall at Westminster). Relations with Magee recovered (Westcott was not a man to bear any grudges), and the humiliation was buried in the record of Westcott's further and triumphant career. But for the contemporary student, it is hard to understand just why involvement in a new and not all that radical version of the Bible might in itself precipitate the decision that someone was too unorthodox to be associated with. I want to look at why such a decision made a kind of sense at the time; and this will open up some reflection on how Westcott approached the Bible, and indeed revelation in general, suggesting a way of understanding different varieties of 'liberalism' within the Anglican theological spectrum – and some thoughts on what has happened lately to that element in the tradition.

By the middle of the nineteenth century, the discoveries of unknown and very ancient witnesses to the biblical text had become fairly common knowledge among the educated public; the discovery and publication of the great codices, Sinaiticus and Vaticanus, during the 1850s and 60s represented the culmination of a long period of textual unsettlement. But to acknowledge that the King James Bible therefore embodied inferior or even mistaken textual traditions was widely seen as an acknowledgement that the authority of the Bible itself was not what it had long been believed to be; to quote Chadwick, 'A sense of insecurity about the Biblical text began to enter some inexpert minds.'[4] If uncertainty were admitted in any area, it infected all – a very familiar anxiety in every modern debate about scriptural authority. The rearguard action against the Revised Version in the 1880s was not simply about issues of style (where there was plenty to criticise) or disinterested scholarship (where there were again some legitimate questions) but drew from the deep well of English biblicism – the conviction, still to be found in some English-speaking Protestant circles, that the 1611 text was the supreme gift of God to Reformed Christianity in the supremely favoured Protestant nation.

Every detail of the text mattered. But the paradox is that Westcott himself believed this with as much passion as any critic of the Revisers. The difference is that for him the problems and uncertainties of the text were themselves *gift*. The Bible is given us by our creator not first as a set of clear narratives and instructions but as something more like a massive canvas depicting the nature of the giver. You need to stand back again and again to see the whole; but you also need to see how that whole is constructed; you have to crawl over its surface inch by inch, not stopping to abstract and frame one section of that surface, but tracing the connections that, detail by detail, make up the whole. Interpretation for the believer is thus a shuttling between the closest possible reading of the text, with all the resources available, and the repeated attempt to find words to articulate the complex unity that is being uncovered.

Chadwick nicely says that Westcott 'loved each word as an individual'.[5] In the course of a twenty-year correspondence with Victoria, Lady Welby, Westcott himself returns to this theme regularly. In 1880, having discussed a number of details in exegesis, he writes, 'These are very small things, yet there is indeed nothing small in Scripture. Every syllable, as Origen said, has, I believe, its force, and the words are living words for us.'[6] And in 1886 he makes the same point in almost the same words: 'I do in my heart believe that every syllable of Holy Scripture, as Origen said, has its work; but I hope I may be saved from the presumption of saying, "It is this, this only".'[7] And the 'work' of each syllable is to provoke us to work. Late in his life, Westcott wrote:

The Bible does not supersede labour, but by its very form proclaims labour to be fruitful . . . There is, no doubt, a restless desire in man for some help which may save him from the painful necessity of reflection, comparison, judgment. But the Bible offers no such help. It offers no wisdom to the careless, and no security to the indolent. It awakens, nerves, invigorates, but it makes no promise of ease.[8]

The invocation of the name of Origen is significant – and Westcott wrote, for the *Dictionary of Christian Biography*, what remains probably the best overview in English of the great Alexandrian's life and work. Origen's conviction of the divine authorship of Scripture was perfectly compatible in his eyes with intensive textual research (according to Eusebius, his sources included what sounds like one of the Dead Sea Scrolls, a text 'found in a jar near Jericho'), a fascination with conflicts and apparent errors in Scripture (as an incentive provided by God to go beyond the surface meaning), and a willingness to sit loose to the historical reference of certain texts. Westcott is cautious about this last (it is illuminating to read in this context the introduction to his commentary on John's Gospel, which will strike the modern student as highly 'conservative'), but the spirit is the same; the fundamental conviction is that Scripture is a field in which to exercise and to grow spiritually. For Origen, exegesis was the attempt to find the unity of divine speech and purpose in the diversity of the text, just as in the diversity of the world;[9] in so doing, the created spirit rediscovered its lost freedom. And for Westcott, the endlessly patient attention to the detail of Scripture makes for human and spiritual maturity; it holds us back from premature and limiting accounts of God's nature and acts. As we read, what we are watching is other human subjects growing by their labour in response to God's initiative; and so we in turn are moved to the same faithful labour and the same patience with mystery. This is not a matter of mystery in the sense of 'new and startling revelations'; we read in the trust that the general sense of the reading Church remains dependable.[10]

But we need to acknowledge that our reading of any one text is likely to be in some degree provisional – simply because we cannot suppose that we shall be able definitively to exhaust what God has given in the whole interactive system of scriptural language and imagery.

This allows Westcott to drive home an important point which may sound surprisingly 'Barthian' for a nineteenth-century Anglican. 'The world is not what I should have expected, nor the Church, nor the Bible.'[11] This emphasis may be in some degree a response not only to conservative Protestant critics, but also to the apriorism of Catholic apologists; Newman's work on development explicitly appeals to what sort of Church we might reasonably expect the saviour to have instituted. But for Westcott, God remains strange to us. In a sermon published in 1884, he writes, in language that might have come from Michael Ramsey:

> The whole record of revelation is a record of the manifestation of God's glory. The Bible is one widening answer to the prayer of Moses, *Show me Thy glory*, which is the natural cry of the soul made for God. The answer does not indeed come as we look for it. We do not understand at first our own weakness. And so God has been pleased to make himself known *in many parts and in many fashions*, by material symbol and through human Presence, as man could bear the knowledge.[12]

To confront the Bible in its entirety is to confront a reality which will continue to surprise us if it is really of God; to systematise it and to idolise the text as a finished set of solutions is to reject the true gift.

To work in faith on the text is to be brought deeper into the unity of all things in Christ. As you might expect, the commentary on John brings this out repeatedly, and one brief passage from the introductory essay sums up much of Westcott's theology.

According to the teaching of St John, the fundamental fact of Christianity includes all that 'is' in each sphere. Christ the Incarnate Word is the perfect revelation of the Father: as God, He reveals God[13]. He is the perfect pattern of life, expressing in act and word the absolute law of love (xiii.34). He unites the finite and the infinite (i.14, xvi.28). And the whole history of the Christian Society is the progressive embodiment of this revelation.'[13]

Here we see clearly the importance for Westcott of faith as incorporation into Christ; perhaps more than any other English writer of the nineteenth century, he defines Christian identity consistently as being where Christ is, in Christ's life and by his power, and all that he has to say, for example, about the atonement is within this context. Another very brief passage, from a letter of 1874 to Lightfoot, spells out the same theological vision as we find in the commentary; the reference is to the Christological hymn at the beginning of Colossians, and Westcott proposes that we read it as alternating between treating the divine Son in relation to creation first as he is in himself, then as he is in virtue of the incarnation. He is the ground of creation as God's eternal image, and 'firstborn' of creation as incarnate.

In short, Westcott is both committed to 'modernity' in the shape of historical study and critical analysis, and strikingly 'pre-modern', as some would define it, in his sense of the near-sacramentality of Scripture. I've mentioned Michael Ramsey as providing something of a parallel in more recent times, but some might also think of Austin Farrer's hermeneutics – Scripture as a scheme of divinely authorised images which we must learn to connect and, in some measure, decode. And both Ramsey and Farrer share with Westcott the quality of being hard to place on many of the conventional maps of liberalism and conservatism. The word 'liberal' was not easy to apply to Westcott, yet there is a sense in which he was seen in such terms by some critics. However, set him alongside Dean Stanley or indeed the authors of *Essays and Reviews*, and the difference is plain. Westcott himself disliked *Essays and Reviews*, and privately expressed himself quite strongly on the subject (see his letters to Hort in August and December 1860;[14] but he was equally dismayed by the opponents of the volume, and briefly considered trying to organise a response from what he considered to be the middle ground, as represented by himself, Lightfoot and Hort. Nothing came of this; but one can sense in some of Westcott's later writing an impatience with the impatience of more systematic liberals. It is noteworthy that Westcott nowhere expresses any misgivings in principle about miracle; and while he clearly understands some of the 'difficulties' (moral and historical) of the Old Testament in the light of a broadly evolutionary theory of religious language and conceptuality, he consistently puts this in the context of the incapacity of the mind to receive truthful impressions of God all at once, without the mediation of personal and historical interaction. His assumption is consistently that the heritage of Christian theology and the credal formularies are 'innocent until proven guilty' – that is, that they should be approached first as possible sources of insight, with something of the same patience that Scripture demands (though it is interesting to see that he takes a strict Reformed line on the eucharistic presence, and finds the *corpus* on a crucifix distracting, since it focuses attention upon the suffering humanity: 'I dare not then rest on this side of the glory' he writes to Lady Welby in 1884.[15]

If Westcott is to be regarded as a liberal, on the grounds at least that he opposed the unthinking hermeneutical literalism of the majority of his fellow-churchmen, we might begin to identify a style of Anglican liberalism that is rather different from what liberalism is commonly supposed to be. The refusal of simple closure in biblical interpretation ('I hope I may be saved from the presumption of saying, "It is this, this only".') is characteristic, of course, of Richard Hooker in his denial of a single identifiable model for Christian ministry in the New Testament; and it is clearly akin to the confessional caution of Sir Thomas Browne and the probabilism of Bishop Butler. It might be summed up as the belief that scriptural and Christian language always says more than it initially seems to say. To believe that you have mastered that 'more' is to arrest a process in which God is actively causing you to grow. Such a perspective in fact entails a very high doctrine of the givenness of Scripture and tradition – even, perhaps, an uncomfortably high doctrine. The agenda set by the media of revelation is not to be negotiated. At the same time, it assumes an interpretative conversation which no one has the right to terminate. The fact that all interlocutors stand before the same data and are not permitted to reduce its agenda, what it 'sets' for exploration, is a qualification of any simplistic approach to authority within the actual practice of interpreting. And for Westcott it is clear, as it was for Origen, that holiness is to be understood as inseparable from this shared practice of 'labour' in the presence of text and tradition. Revelation provides not a system to be received but a language in which to discover more and more echoes and consonances.

This is not an easy model to define with precision. We are so used to connecting belief in the divine origin or authorisation of Scripture with belief in inerrancy or something similar that it is surprising to see in Westcott – as, once again, in Origen – a passionate belief in the divine *purpose* somehow at work in 'every syllable' of the Bible combined with a sensitivity to genre, to human creativity in the composition of the Bible and to the imperative of reading the text as a whole. But for Westcott, the simple traditionalist position of his day, the position of the critics of *Essays and Reviews* (especially the bishops), failed to make the all-important connection between the character of Scripture and the character of growth in participation in Christ. In one of his more popular and direct meditations on the resurrection, *The Revelation of the Risen Lord*,[16] he takes the Emmaus narrative as summing up the active and mobile presence of the risen Christ in the believer's life, walking with us in the process of our doubt and our discovery alike.[17] The resurrection life in Christ is irreducibly a matter of searching; and the Bible itself is the narrative of the fundamental paradox that we search because we have already been found. If we seek for closure in hermeneutics and theology, we step away from the Emmaus road. The certainty we may have in committing ourselves to Scripture and the creeds is not in the possession of solutions but in the almost 'marital' promise to abide with this language and framework for our growing. In his 1883 lectures on the Apostles' Creed,[18] he very typically takes Romans 6:17 and turns upside down the traditional translation: it is not that a form of teaching has been delivered to us, but that *we* have been 'delivered to the doctrine'. We have been placed within a new sphere of experience, new impressions and forces summed up in the language of Scripture and creed.

If I may pick up here a distinction I have tried to elaborate elsewhere,[19] this approach corresponds quite closely to one of the two varieties of 'scepticism' regularly found in Anglican literature, a scepticism about formulae and dogma that is fundamentally scepticism about the capacities of the human mind. It assumes that we are liable to self-deceit, that our knowledge is affected by our moral and spiritual lack. In this context, to be cautious about hermeneutical or dogmatic closure is not to discard or relativise sanctioned words; you occupy the territory marked out by those words, but you will not know where the boundaries are, because the search for definite boundaries suggests that you might be 'in possession' of the territory, not yourself included in (possessed by?) it. And this contrasts with a scepticism more obviously generated by Enlightenment suspicion of authority, in which the target of the questioning is the formulae as such and the processes by which they were shaped. To revert for a moment to a phrase used a little while ago, this would be a conviction that Christian language says *less* than it claims to say; that it encodes illegitimate claims and covert appeals to uncriticised power. If we want to identify a genealogy within Anglicanism for this kind of scepticism, we might look to Bishop Hoadly's relentless deconstruction of eucharistic imagery in the early eighteenth century (what can possibly be 'happening' in the Eucharist that is not a mental process on our part?); perhaps to *Essays and Reviews* itself. It is worth noting that Westcott as a young man certainly did not see either Arnold or Hampden as alien to his own understanding,[20] and was still writing of Arnold with warmth and respect in 1872.[21] It would be interesting to trace the two 'routes' out of Arnold's heritage that issued in a Westcott on the one hand and a Stanley on the other; Westcott was generally on good terms with Stanley, and distinguished his views from those of Jowett,[22] but their attitudes to exegesis were widely different, and Stanley was not happy about altering the King James Bible. Both may have been, in the eyes of some, 'broad' in their ecclesiastical allegiance, but Stanley's anecdotal and sentimental approach to both Scripture and doctrine does not sit easily with Westcott's intensity of meditation. But we must assume that Westcott found in Arnold and Stanley alike something of the same reverent awkwardness before the language of Scripture and creeds that characterised his own method.

Westcott's 'liberalism' is the claim of a liberty *within* the given structures of Bible and doctrine to decline closure: these are the words we cannot but use, but we cannot prescribe precisely how they are to be understood, because just that is the unending 'labour' which is God's gift to us through the medium of this sacred vocabulary. In that sense it is distinct from the claim to renegotiate the language itself, on the grounds that it asserts more than the post-Enlightenment mind can cope with. The former, you might say, takes seriously at more than one level the importance of time for understanding: that is, it begins by recognising the time taken in the formation of scriptural and doctrinal words, and assumes that further time requires to be taken in grasping them. Its approach to the tradition (including the text of Scripture) is very much that of a native speaker of the language, testing its possibilities. Westcott was, predictably, an admirer of Browning; and there would be some intriguing work to do on this relationship, on the sense in which Browning as a religious, indeed a doctrinally confessional, poet might be seen as mirroring something of Westcott's methodology. Certainly, to put side by side Westcott's John commentary and Browning's still astonishing and stretching *A Death in the Desert* makes the point:

> Then stand before that fact, that Life and Death,
> Stay there at gaze, till it dispart, dispread,
> As though a star should open out, all sides,
> And grow the world on you, as it is my world.

It would be hard to find a better metaphor for Westcott's exegesis.

In contrast, what I have characterised as the more unproblematic affirmations of modernity or Enlightenment in other writers risks a more dismissive attitude to the taking of time. There can be an assumption that scriptural or doctrinal language stands before us as straightforwardly the product of a process now definitively past. These were the constraints that moved our ancestors to say this; such are not our constraints, and so we cannot say this. And this will tend to neglect the unfinished business of the tradition's language, the questions and issues raised in a process that does not find a simple closure in the production of the formulae. When that unfinished business is recognised, Scripture and creed become something more like reports on where the labour has arrived so far within a project that continues. It becomes less easy to set a self-enclosed modernity over against a self-enclosed pre-modernity.

What I am trying to define here is that strand in Anglican 'liberalism' that is content to inhabit the linguistic and imaginative world given by the interweaving of history and grace; its concern is not to renegotiate boundaries but to turn the soil of tradition within what has been received. If we look for more recent successors of Westcott, I suspect we shall find them less in the sphere of exegesis, let alone systematics, than among the hard-to-categorise explorers who work on the borderlines of spirituality and philosophy or the arts or sciences: Vanstone, obviously, and Ecclestone, but also John Bowker or John Drury; among a younger generation, Mark Oakley. If we look back a little to the history of twentieth-century theology, we might think of that doyen of a certain style of Catholic liberalism, Alec Vidler; perhaps the earlier writings of Harry Williams. John Robinson is intriguing in this connection as someone who seemed to move from a more generally Enlightenment and revisionist style in *Honest to God* towards something closer to Westcott in his later works, most of all in his last ten years (*Truth is Two-Eyed* and the final clutch of New Testament and doctrinal essays – not to mention his labours on the fourth gospel). Ulrich Simon, a scourge of what he thought of as liberalism, especially the early Robinson's, might, paradoxically, be included in this lineage; as might R. S. Thomas – those two names just to remind us that the tragic sense is not so absent in this world as is sometimes assumed. Those who look at Westcott's own theology primarily through the lens of the *Christus Consummator* language he so loved have missed something, the element that takes his thinking beyond a spiritually intensified culture-Protestantism: consider the implication of another of Westcott's 'throwaway' remarks in commenting on John 12:27 ('Now is my soul troubled'), where he simply notes that this troubled soul is that 'in which was gathered up the fulness of present human life'.[23]

But at this point we had better beware of that perennial Anglican temptation to identify a genealogy of 'real' Anglican doctors and masters or mistresses, and to refuse to do exactly what the very methodology outlined here prescribes – that is, to look carefully at what prompts and animates the 'labour' of the Enlightenment, modernist critic. I suggested a little while back that the ethos I have been discussing is marked by scepticism not about tradition or authority as such but about human capacity and the reach of language; while the scepticism of the other voice in the story is directed more against claims to authority and assumptions about what is non-negotiably given, since such claims encode significant messages concerning power. Westcottian liberalism can become more than faintly self-indulgent, almost an aesthetic of belief, leaving to others the different kind of labour that has to come to

terms with serious public conflict and the risks of loss. Where
the language of Scripture and tradition is seen not just as hazily
unfinished and inviting but as intellectually or morally destructive,
the issues are harder. To put it very concretely, Westcott's approach
to the first stirrings of women's emancipation, in education and
society at large (he opposed the granting of degrees to women),
leaves some considerable unease; and while his commitment to
'Christian Socialism' was clear, many commentators have asked
whether it amounted to more than commending a transformation
of the way the system worked rather than of the system itself. In
our contemporary setting, Westcott alone will not greatly help us,
at first sight, with the Anglican Communion's embarrassed and
ungraceful debates about sexuality and authority.

Two observations here. First, and more simply, Westcott's
concern to see the whole picture in the labour of exegesis does
allow a critical principle to enter the discussion of any one issue.
Secondly, and following from this, we might want to say that what
the study of the 'labour' of Bible and doctrine shows us is that
this sense of the wholeness of the picture is going to alter, sometimes quite significantly, from generation to generation. The canon
itself shows the signs of this shifting sense of what wholeness is.
Without, then, the overt challenges, the voices of protest and
impatience, the givenness of Scripture and creed becomes a temptation to complacency; and Westcott's own theological assumption
that the Word was at work beyond ecclesial boundaries certainly
licenses an openness to the Enlightenment agenda in the process
of reshaping what we imagine the strongest contours of the wider
landscape to be.

I am not recommending that we resolve or remove the tensions
between two varieties of 'liberalism' by deciding that there is a
'good' tradition and a 'bad' one (Westcott versus Jowett, say, or
Alec Vidler versus Bishop Barnes). But I am pleading for a recognition on all sides that the word 'liberalism' is complex and slippery,
and that, despite the angry polemic of the right, there is no single
'liberal agenda' to be written off as apostasy. But on the other

side, I want to pose some questions to an ecclesial left that can collude with the conservative caricature by assuming that there is indeed a self-evident emancipatory agenda, in which all issues can be decided by appeal to a particular definition of rights. An approach informed by Westcott might say that this too easily allows doctrine to be shaped by apologetics of a certain kind and avoids the labour of working through why a new perspective on some questions remains part of one continuing conversation, part of a common work with the writers of the Bible or the creeds. Which is why it is worth trying to exhibit what in Scripture or doctrine might suggest that – say – the emancipation of women is something to do with the opening out of the one star that Browning writes of – with the consequent admission that what had been thought the clear contours of the map have been in some ways misrecognised. But this is unlikely to happen until the questions of emancipationist modernity have been listened to without panic and rejection.

SIX

MICHAEL RAMSEY
(1904–1988)

Theology and the Churches

Christian theology is not only a detached exercise of the Christian intellect; it is the life of the one Body in which Truth is both thought out and lived out.[1]

Under modern conditions I think a theologian has got to be a heretic. The relation between religious belief and modern culture is so extreme you have to be innovative and exploratory. You have to be all the things that Michael Ramsey abhorred.[2]

TWO RADICALLY DIFFERENT judgements on the nature of theology, one from Ramsey himself, one from the doyen of contemporary Anglican 'heretics', Don Cupitt. How are such judgements formed, and how should both Church and academy think now about theology? What I want to suggest here is that how you think about theology, how you make your judgements as to what kind of an enterprise it is, how you conceive its relation to the life of the churches, actually depends, in the long run, on how you are thinking about the Church in the first place. This may sound a bit circular: what we say about theology depends on our theology of the Church. However, I have in mind not so much some sort of 'given' doctrine of the Church but rather the underlying, imperfectly voiced assumptions as to the sort of thing the Church is – which, in turn, reflect the underlying assumptions as to the nature of what (if anything) is done for us in the events of Jesus' life and death. Ramsey, above all in that abiding classic, *The Gospel and the Catholic Church*, stands within a broad trend in Anglican, Roman Catholic and Orthodox thinking in the last century which seeks to articulate one particular sense of what the Church is; a sense which is currently much in eclipse in two of those traditions and often rather distorted in the third; a sense, too, which is obscured by both self-consciously traditionalist and self-consciously liberal theologians at present. The perspective expressed by Don Cupitt's remarks, on the other hand, expresses a sense of the Church's identity that is substantially and, I think, irreconcilably different. The question we are left with in investigating these two approaches is whether, finally, we have to stand with either Ramsey or Cupitt; whether the sense Ramsey works with is part of the necessary common sense of the Church, without which theology, worship, ecumenism, whatever, are going to be empty.

Ramsey's first book was far from uncontroversial when it appeared in 1936.[3] It was regarded with dismay by many in Ramsey's former (and future) university as another example of the malign influence of foreign irrationalism – the new Protestant orthodoxy of Barth, especially – just as much as an example of ecclesiastical rigidity: *theologians* ought not to waste their time writing about liturgy and things like that.[4] It is perhaps easier now than, say, thirty years ago to understand the depth of feeling that could pervade debates about the place and authority of revelation in theology at a time when the faltering responses of classical liberalism to the horrors of war and totalitarianism had prompted a good many to despair of any kind of common rationality as a tool, let alone a source, for theology. Today a similar debate continues, with some of the same intensity of feeling, over whether theology has a 'rationality' proper to itself in a world where, once again, the resources of liberalism are running thin; but now the situation is further complicated by the intellectual importance of a 'post-modern' milieu that is sceptical of *any* universalising intellectual projects, and at times seems to relish the prospect of a tribalising of intellectual life.[5] Ramsey's book represents what was to become a more and more powerful and popular option in certain Anglican circles over the decade that followed its first publication. It takes up the challenges posed by his mentor Edwyn Hoskyns both in the latter's own work and in his translation of Barth's second commentary on Romans:[6] challenges that might be summarised as forcing upon the rather comfortable world of Anglican philosophical theology the imperative of rediscovering a theology of the cross. The very first chapter of *The Gospel and the Catholic Church* (entitled 'The Passion and the Church Today') sets the tone very clearly: the problems of the Church, not least problems of reunion between Christians, cannot be met, or even intelligently thought about, unless it is recognised that the Church exists because of the death and resurrection of Jesus, and that any project in which the Church approaches more nearly to 'becoming what it is' (not Ramsey's phrase) involves sacrifice, dispossession. All projects and ideals, theological, spiritual, intellectual, social, must go into the melting-pot under the imperative of the cross of God incarnate. It is no accident that, in later chapters,[7] some of Ramsey's most impassioned writing is devoted to Luther – not such a very common bedfellow for a Catholic Anglican divine (then or now).[8]

This alignment with the demands of the cross brought with it a consciously rhetorical and often paradoxical style. It was to be echoed in other writers of the same tendency: think of the extremism, what one commentator has called the 'brutality', of Donald MacKinnon's early theological essays, which undoubtedly owe much to Hoskyns and Ramsey.[9] The vision seems to dictate a strong note of extremism, indeed, of what the same commentator has called 'impossibilism':[10] the Church, in common with the whole redemptive process, does not exist as the fruit of human endeavour, which is shown time and again by the bloody collapse of 'civilised' rationality to be incapable of attaining anything that is lastingly healing. Thus the Church cannot be reformed by human effort and ingenuity, any more than sin can be eradicated by good will. We must hear the gospel of the incarnation as a summons to self-abandonment before all else, not as a reassuring endorsement of the best we can humanly do. In the light of this, it is odd to see Ramsey, here as elsewhere, giving so much house room to F.D. Maurice, whose theological interest in what a later German generation was to reject as 'creation ordinances' independent of the gospel (the organic structures of nation, community and family) seems so much at odds with the theology of the cross that dominates most of Ramsey's first book. Indeed, the passages in which Ramsey attempts to show that Maurice too sees the disruptive cross at the centre of theology[11] fall some way short of a persuasive argument: Maurice certainly stresses the need for the Church to put the atonement at the heart of its preaching, but is more interested in the *completeness* of what has been achieved in the sacrifice of Christ than in the Christian appropriation of the way of the cross.[12]

If we ask, however, why Ramsey should have found Maurice so sympathetic (and it was not an affinity he ever forswore),[13] the answer in fact tells us much about the central and controlling vision that animates *The Gospel and the Catholic Church*, and thus about what Ramsey thought theology was. Maurice is profoundly concerned (as few if any theologians of his or Ramsey's generation were) with the centrality of *trinitarian* theology; and he also (again in a way not easy to parallel in other writers of the age) grants a place of the highest significance in theological method to the language of the Church's public worship. In short, Maurice was concerned to understand the Church's life as something in which *the nature of God was made manifest*; and this was close enough to Ramsey's animating enthusiasms to make of Maurice an ally against both the liberalism he and Maurice rejected so passionately, and the conservatism that saw the Church as fundamentally a divinely organised institution, whose structures were given under law. If we now read Maurice a little more suspiciously,[14] noting the hierarchical assumptions that sit comfortably unquestioned in his social thought and his theological positivism about the state as divinely instituted, we should remember that in Ramsey's day critical discussion of Maurice – indeed, discussion of any kind regarding his work – was in its infancy. For most of those who bothered to read him at all, he had something of the same liberating impact as he obviously had in Ramsey's case: he was heard, rightly, as a voice breaking through some sterile oppositions between Protestant and Catholic loyalties.

This third way opened up the minds of many Anglicans to a perspective that was beginning to appear in continental Catholicism and was being introduced into the ecumenical scene largely by émigré Russian writers.[15] It is essentially the vision of the Church as 'epiphany': what matters about the Church is not a system of ideas as such (though doctrine and dogma have their place) nor the structure of an organisation competent to deliver authoritative judgements and to require obedience (though order is important in its proper context), but what the bare fact of the Church *shows*. *The Gospel and the Catholic Church* sets out first to determine the shape of divine action (gift, sacrifice, the creation of a qualitatively new human fellowship) and then to demonstrate how doctrine and discipline in the Catholic tradition make present and tangible the pattern of divine action. In an unusually sharp couple of sentences on Calvin and the weaknesses of his theology of the Christian community,[16] Ramsey expresses very clearly what he believes matters most for the Church:

> For Calvin, however, the Church is rather utilitarian. It is not perceived as the glow of Christ's incarnate presence; it is the policeman sent to protect the Christian life by commands and prohibitions. Here is discipline, without the sense of union with the death and life of Christ which gives discipline its

meaning; here is order, without the sense of the wondrous historical and apostolic race which gives order its meaning.

I suspect that Ramsey is really doing what he generally says should not be done – treating a theology of ministry as a theology of the Church, castigating Calvin for not retaining the sense of Catholic order in his functionalist remoulding of the Christian ministry. Others would want to defend Calvin's *overall* theology of the worshipping community as far closer to Ramsey's ideal. However, the point is that Ramsey has already elaborated at length his reasons for believing that the traditional Catholic order is not an alien superstructure imposed on a 'message', but is actually the *language* in which that message is communicable in its fullness. Furthermore, he does, in effect, grant in his earlier pages about the medieval Church that Calvin and others could be forgiven for missing the point in the climate of their own day.

Fundamentally, however, the Church *is* the message. There is no cluster of ideas or ideals that can be abstracted from the life of the Church and passed on in some sort of neutral medium; to belong in the Church is to know what God wants you to know, because it is to live as God wants you to live. But this is where we need to read carefully. Put as baldly as that – God wants you to belong to the Church – Ramsey's vision is not only unattractive, it could be read as a call to conformism or submission to an institutional authority. This is what it would mean if the Church were here being defined as a society devoted to promoting certain kinds of behaviour or ideas as specified by an expert élite or governing caste; and much of the tragedy of the Church's history derives from the fact that this is exactly how the Church has appeared at various times. Ramsey has hard words for the doctrine of papal authority because it defines the unity of the Church in terms of a unity of 'executive' power: there is one supreme legitimate source for imperatives in faith and morals, and belonging in the Church is equivalent to submission to this.[17] Not much better is what Ramsey sees as the Protestant distortion that appears to understand unity in terms either of what can be enforced by the biblically educated pastors of the community (as in his characterisation of Calvin already quoted) or of shared feelings.[18] But the true Church does not exist for the sake of advancing something other than its own integrity – whether it is a system of authoritative teaching or a set of sentiments. It is first and foremost the epiphany of God's action, especially God's action in the paschal events, and so too of God's nature. It exists to radiate the glory of God.

This can only be seriously maintained, of course, if we allow that the Church is what it is visibly and tangibly in one specific context – the Eucharist. This is not an arbitrary stipulation. If what it is to be a Christian is to be 'in Christ', the community of Christians is what it is only in so far as it is in Christ, united with Christ's divine action. It is itself where human beings renounce their private and protected selfhoods 'in a death like his', so that their self-emptying mirrors the self-emptying of God the Word in Jesus' life and death. Considered as a narrative about human biographies, this process of self-emptying is always going to be flawed and incomplete, vulnerable to corruption and failure. Yet the Church is not, in the New Testament, simply a project initiated by Jesus and struggling to achieve its destiny; it exists in its fullness, it is already the community of those who are holy and who bear the identity of Christ. Thus the Church is itself precisely where it is transparent to the divine action – which means that the Church is itself in the sacraments. Here the diversity of human biographies is traced back to its source in the act of God, and the diversity of Christian biographies is traced back to the one unrepeatable event of Good Friday and Easter; the Church's unity is 'in a real sense a sharing in those events'[19] and so in the single coherent divine action that eternally underlies and makes sense of the paschal story. Baptism inaugurates the reality of a life that can be transparent to God; but the rite that *manifests* all this repeatedly, publicly, corporately is the Eucharist. Here 'It is still the Messiah who gives thanks and breaks bread'; and the eucharistic liturgy 'is not only the most important of a series of rites, but the divine act into which all prayers and praises are drawn'.[20] In such a context, the ordained ministry of the Church is simply what serves to show the full meaning of the sacramental assembly: that it is united in time to the events of Easter and that it lives always by a life that is not and could not be restricted to a local or sectional or national context. The Catholic ministry is a mark of the kenotic structure of the Church's life, the fundamental truth that no person or specific community lives of, by or for itself.

Such is the apostolic function as the New Testament seems to envisage it;[21] and this, Ramsey argues eloquently in the sixth chapter of *The Gospel and the Catholic Church*, is exactly what episcopacy now expresses in the Catholic Church. The bishop or his deputy presiding at the assembly of the Church in order to let the Messiah act, in order to bring the prayers of the Christian people into unity with the self-offering in time and eternity of Christ the High Priest,[22] is part of the way in which the Church, simply by being what it is, communicates the glory of God. The presence of the ordained is not dictated by juridical requirements or by some theory of occult powers granted only to the clergy. They are there presiding in the assembly in order to show some-thing – the unity of the Church in the cross and resurrection of Jesus. Without the apostolic ministry, the problem is not a defect of 'validity' in the usual Catholic sense but a defect of clarity and intelligibility in the symbolic communication of the gospel of God. The liturgy becomes a performance of a choral work with one whole vocal part missing – not quite *Hamlet* without the Prince, but the harmony without the sopranos, perhaps.

This is one of the points where Ramsey is probably closest to some of his Orthodox friends and mentors. It is noteworthy that such discussion as there is in the Russian Orthodox works Ramsey would have read on the subject of ordained ministry concentrates heavily on the 'epiphanic' role of the clergy,[23] not on their power of rule or their pastoral or teaching task. If you want to know what clergy are for, do not start with pragmatic considerations, the jobs you would like clergy to do in running things or providing 'leadership' (not a word you would expect Ramsey to relish in a book focusing so closely on the priority of the cross); start with the *picture* of an assembly that in its formal structure and its disposition of responsibilities and its language, gesture and process draws you towards a contemplative understanding of the act of God in cross and resurrection and in the eternal love by which God is God. You could, I think, quite reasonably ask of Ramsey's model (as some have asked of Orthodox models) whether *this* Church exists, practically speaking, between celebrations of the Eucharist, or even whether the ordained should have any specific responsibilities other than the conduct of the epiphanic liturgy. I suspect that Ramsey's answer to that would probably be in elaborating what it is to be given the sort of 'guardianship' of the Church's unity in the cross that is spelled out in the chapters on order in general and bishops in particular. It is also, of course, given concretely and unforgettably in his masterpiece of practical pastoral theology, *The Christian Priest Today*; but that takes us into rather different territory.

Now the point of this brief overview of the themes of Ramsey's first book is to indicate what is being taken for granted in the comment on theology with which this chapter began. We could sum this up by saying that it depends on a distinctive view of truth itself, truth as *appropriate relation to reality* at every level. We habitually assume that the only appropriate relation that matters is the supposed correspondence of words to things; but this is increasingly inadequate both as a theological and as a philosophical foundation, or so we have been told by a good many recent writers.[24] Ramsey, in his ninth chapter, elaborates what he describes as the 'biblical' model of truth: truth is 'a quality of the living God in action', and thus appears as 'God's saving plan as He rules in history'.[25] Consequently, we know it in so far as we are taken into the shape and movement of that action – which means in turn that it cannot be apprehended without repentance and transfiguration. This is how what Scripture calls 'wisdom' is imparted, giving to us the light in which we are to interpret the whole range of our human environment.[26] Yet again, Ramsey is best read alongside some of the major Orthodox theologians of the century: Florovsky, certainly, but more recently John Zizioulas, who has developed the theme of the inseparability of 'Truth and Communion' (the title of a major essay that deserves a paper to itself).[27] Here we find a stress not so much on the characteristically sub-Barthian idea of the truth as the act of God which appears in Ramsey, but on truth as itself that indestructible life that is open to us when we cease to live as private and self-determining individuals and enter the communion of the Church's life, which is also the communion of God's own personal life-in-relation. And, since Zizioulas links this very directly to the Eucharist,[28] the parallel with Ramsey is very close indeed.

The role of theology, then, is strictly unintelligible in such a context if it once ceases to be reflection on *relations* that have been established by something other than an individual intellect – the relation of our words to God's act and our *acts* to God's act which is imparted in the liturgy and made possible by the incarnation, death and resurrection of the Word, and then the relation of Christian persons to one another in a community that is never simply an association of individuals with interests in common. The norms and limits of theology are thus set not by the decree of an external authority (and we could look again here at Ramsey's hostile pages on papal authoritarianism) but by the logic of these relations. That is to say, theology would simply stop being itself if it abandoned the belief that in Jesus God had acted to reconstruct the bonds that unite humanity and connect it with the source of divine life; or even if it redefined the Eucharist as an aid to individual devotion or a ceremony expressive of deep feelings of human solidarity. A theologian who went down such paths would not be doing bad or even heretical theology; she or he would not be doing theology at all, merely a no doubt respectable and disciplined and serious form of independent religious reflection on the social patterns of a community whose origins and meaning could be adequately accounted for in straightforwardly historical terms. If this is right, then for Ramsey – as, I think, for Hooker[29] – there cannot but be some grey areas in the detail of dogmatic teaching (not least about the structures of Church and ministry); but what remains non-negotiable is the central complex of commitments which depend on a belief that God acts to renew the divine image, in person and community, through Jesus. Ramsey's initially hostile response to *Honest to God*, a response which he later regretted somewhat, has about it a sense of disquiet at the dismissal not of insupportable ideas but of deep-rooted idioms of prayer.[30] While Ramsey undoubtedly found it hard to see exactly what doctrine of God and Christ John Robinson was advancing, his chief anxiety was to do with what he clearly thought to be Robinson's 'tone-deafness' as to the language of piety. It is not fair to say, as has been said,[31] that Ramsey was wholly unreceptive to new theological ideas, though his reading was not much less restricted than that of most bishops tends to become after a few years (shades of the prison-house . . .). He did, however, take it for granted that there was a focus to Christian belief and practice which, precisely because it was not a matter of conceptual structures, but a multiple and elusive sense of the divine action in Jesus and the worshipping community, was simply not vulnerable to intellectual or cultural fashion – and to speak or write as if it were would be to stop doing theology, to turn to one's own agenda as the subject-matter of religious reflection. In so far as Ramsey thought again about *Honest to God*, it was surely because he recognised, as have several generations of readers, that the conceptually troubled waters at the surface of the book conceal a commitment as strong in many ways as Ramsey's own to the vision of a new humanity in Christ, realised in the eucharistic assembly.

Yet this particular case focuses the kind of difficulty felt even by the most sympathetic contemporary reader of Ramsey. If you begin by taking for granted the historic community, liturgy and hierarchy of the Church, if this is to be the context and the test for all theological utterance, are we not faced with the danger that theology becomes the self-justification of the Church, an ideology of ecclesiastical power? The account of the role of bishops in the Church, for instance, is eloquent and even compelling in terms of epiphany and symbolism; but we must surely also be aware of what it means and has always meant in terms of the concrete exercise of power. Does the history of ecclesiastical hierarchy allow us to speak so serenely about what is made manifest in the eucharistic assembly? We have been urged all too often in recent years to reread much of early Christian history as a history of struggles for ideological dominance;[32] and if theology is defined as reflection on the epiphany of God's character in the hierarchically organised assembly, it will be in danger of burying a great deal of history. It might be just as theological (or even *more* theological) to reflect on the history of struggle, power and exclusion in the Church. The theologies that now come from those who have experienced this history of exclusion, women especially, ought surely to have some claim to count as authentic, a 'living out of Truth' in the life of the Body.

This is, I believe, a fair objection, as it is to some styles of Orthodox theology. A faith in which historical narration is fundamental can hardly afford to conceal its own history when it reflects on its nature and calling. Ramsey, of course, does engage with some aspects of the history of the Church in the last few chapters of *The Gospel and the Catholic Church*, but there is a tendency here for the discussion to slip into a kind of intellectual history dominated by 'ideal types' (as witness his account of Calvinism, already referred to), and innocent of contextual problems (as in the discussion of F. D. Maurice). He was, of course, writing at a time when this particular kind of ideological suspiciousness was by no means a regular part of the intellectual historian's equipment. Certainly, Ramsey enlarges at length upon the 'perversions' of Western Christianity in the medieval period, but this is always in terms of a decline from the golden age of the Fathers, which is not itself subjected to critical historical analysis. It cannot be denied that all this constitutes a weakness in the style of theology advocated and embodied in *The Gospel*. When all this is granted, however, there is a crucially important counter-point to be made. If the theologies that emerge from the experience of the victimised and excluded, the theologies that deploy suspicion and ideological critique, are to be in any sense *theology*, not just the expression of an assortment of resentments, they are bound to work with a governing critical model of what the Body might be. They become a manifestation of the life of the Body as a *thinking* life to the extent that they continue to pose as the ultimate critical point of reference a system of relations between persons established by the events of revelation – that is, by the history of Israel and Jesus. Without this, a purportedly critical theology can become an uncritical deployment of whatever are supposed to be the most obvious and socially accessible models of the good life at any given time. What I called earlier in this essay 'the faltering responses of classical liberalism' to the crisis of public values in the 1930s are as inadequate now as then.

In a much-quoted and haunting phrase,[33] Ramsey speaks of what the Catholic Church 'learns and re-learns in humiliation': 'Catholicism always stands before the church door at Wittenberg to read the truth by which she is created and by which also she is judged.' Perhaps we best understand the critical resources of Ramsey's theology in the light of a remark like this. The Church must always be looking at and appropriating its own historical failure; in so far as 'Wittenberg' represents (for Ramsey) a moment when the Catholic tradition is challenged to acknowledge its failure, it articulates a principle of basic theological importance. The Church lives under judgement: its empirical condition is always to be thought through, tested in the light of the reality to which its existence is supposed to bear witness. While the normal manifestation of that reality is the sacramental life of the eucharistic assembly, there are times when this has to be activated in the imagination and consciousness of the Church by history itself, by moments of rupture and protest. But *if* the Church has actually been paying attention to the substance of its sacramental life, it ought to be able to interpret such historical moments correctly, and so to 'learn in humiliation'.

In other words, I think Ramsey is granting implicitly that what might seem like a disturbingly seamless and epiphanic model of the Church, timelessly showing forth in its liturgy and hierarchy the mystery of God's nature, will not tell us the whole story. If we understand what it means to enact in worship the pattern of God's kenosis, the costly mutuality that is established by the death and resurrection of Jesus, and the universal horizon of God's work in Christ, we should be on the watch constantly for the kind of ideological bondage that threatens to take over a Church-based or Church-focused theology. But the liturgy is, humanly speaking, administered and actualised by fallible human agents, who are all enmeshed in relations other than those of the redeemed community, and who thus constantly introduce such alien patterns into the Church, even when presiding at the eucharistic assembly, the eschatological congregation of God's people bonded in charity. This is why it will not do to have a theology of ordained ministry that is entirely based on their epiphanic role, however important it may be to redress the balance against managerial and governmental models. The Church may be perfectly the Church at the Eucharist, but its life is not exhausted in the Eucharist: there is a life that is always struggling to realise outside the 'assembly' what the assembly shows forth.[34] In that context, theology requires the angry and sometimes disruptive gestures of history, requires the naming of 'humiliation', in order to recognise the prophetic import of what it does in worship, especially when even worship in its presentation or structure at any one time may speak of injustices or betrayals of the gospel (as when the ordained ministry speaks of one or another kind of social exclusion, when ceremonial speaks of anxiety or servility, when language evokes alienating or oppressive images).

Ramsey, in short, is difficult to claim for either reaction or radicalism as normally understood. But – to return to the antithesis with which I began this chapter – he would not, I think, have seen the point of defining the theologian's task as necessarily heretical. The tension for him is not between 'religious belief' and 'modern culture' as two systems of thought, but rather between the form of corporate human life realised through Christ and the Spirit in the eucharistic assembly and all other forms of human sociality. Furthermore, this is a tension (not, of course, an absolute opposition) that is not to be resolved by thinking, by conceptual readjustments. Where there is a crisis of plausibility, where the Church is manifestly alienated from the currents of contemporary reflection and perception, the exploratory religious thinking of an individual is *not* of necessity the way to overcome it. In Ramsey's frame of reference, what needs doing is a mutual probing by Church and not-Church, a reciprocal testing of honesty and resource, which cannot be reduced to a programme of revisionism. For a theologian to try to test the integrity of his or her world of religious discourse requires a fundamental commitment to that world as deserving of attention, as having depths worth sounding, even when the surface language is muddled or obscure, just as much as it demands an attention to the forms of social construction and the cultural voices that currently prevail. It demands a belief that the life of the Body can appropriately be 'thought', and not only lived unreflectively or uncritically. Yet this in turn takes it for granted that there is some 'pre-understanding' of the distinctiveness of the Body itself – which can only be nurtured by the distinctive common practices of the Body, by worship and the daily struggles for holiness and justice in human affairs. When Bonhoeffer, in his unforgettable letter to his godson of May 1944,[35] spoke of the failures of religious words to transform the world, he envisaged a time when Christian self-awareness would have to remain content with 'prayer and righteous action', living in expectancy of a rebirth of words gifted with presence and power. Ramsey's style of theologising is about as different as could be from Bonhoeffer's, but, to the extent that Ramsey stresses the Church's need to learn in 'humiliation', to be brought to silence before what has created it, he may point us to the same place.

Some things must be shown not spoken, or shown before spoken; or the speaking has to be absorbed again and again into the showing. A Church without the thinking and speaking of the underlying nature of its common life is in danger of muffling the critical energy that is in reality always at work in it; a theology without anchorage in the showing of God's life that is the Church's liturgy becomes uncritical in a different way, talkative and bold in its own sophistications. To say that Ramsey's is the only rationale, finally, for a theology that does not turn into religious phenomenology is not a recipe for repetitious ideology and obedient intellectual idleness in the Church; simply an acknowledgement that, if there is anything at all to be said for understanding the gospel as a gift, and, more specifically, a gift in the form of a remaking of human bonds, theology will always be stumbling to keep up with something prior. That is both its privilege and its cross, articulating (from the theologian's own experience in the Church) the 'learning in humiliation', learning in the failure and impotence of formulae, that returns the Church to its source.

SEVEN

JOHN A.T. ROBINSON
(1919–1983)

Honest to God and the 1960s

I T WAS A MOST UNLIKELY best-seller. It assumed that its readers would know at least something about the intellectual history of modern Europe (names like those of Kant and Feuerbach are introduced summarily, as if we would at least have heard of them before); it uses, again and again, a tone of relentless abstraction and a string of semitechnical words (supranaturalism, theonomy, secularity . . .); and, above all, its central thesis is elusive almost to disappearing point. To call it a 'work which almost anyone could read', as does Adrian Hastings in his *History of English Christianity 1920–1990*, is a bit optimistic.[1] And, as unfriendly critics pointed out, Robinson's characteristic style is to present a startling caricature of traditional doctrine, apologise for overstating his case, and offer a rather dense translation into his preferred idiom, which leaves the reader unclear as to quite what status is now being ascribed either to the language with which we began or to the new version offered by the author. The pervasive problem is whether Robinson's translations effectively render the doctrinal scheme no more than a complex metaphor for different kinds of experienced *intensity.*

So it is instructive to look, in this light, at one particular review of the book, and at Robinson's reaction to it. The young Alasdair

MacIntyre was at that point in his intellectual odyssey very consciously post-Christian and post-Marxist; he had written in the early 1950s a beautifully concise and clear book on Christianity and Marxism, at a time when, he says, he 'aspired to be both a Christian and a Marxist', but had moved away, into a constructive and very interesting scepticism about 'the relation of belief to organisation'.[2] Fifteen years on from the book's first publication, he notes the way in which the Christian and the Marxist frameworks obstinately survive what some think to be decisive refutation, and the relative blindness both systems share as to the degree and nature of their own conditionedness, their clumsiness in telling the difference between their fundamental insights and those aspects of their discourses that are 'defensive or aggressive responses to their social situation'.[3]

These, then, were the issues preoccupying MacIntyre in the early 1960s; and from this perspective he begins his review, memorably, with the words: 'What is striking about Dr. Robinson's book is first and foremost that he is an atheist.'[4] He is able, without too much difficulty, to show that Robinson repeatedly uses language whose plain meaning is that theology seeks to describe what human beings are and no more; but he goes on to ask the deeper question of whether modern Protestant theology is 'essentially atheistic'.[5] His answer is twofold: The apparently more traditional idiom of Karl Barth at the very least runs the risk of leaving huge vulnerabilities exposed because it insists that we cannot argue but only submit to the divine Word. If theology is therefore bound to fail, if the divine Word is wholly unsayable in human language, what really remains? And this leads to the second wing of the argument: What replaces theology is a rhetoric of moral seriousness, as in Tillich, for whom the real subject of theological assertions is the human psyche.

But the most searching of MacIntyre's observations relates to Bonhoeffer. When all else fails, the integrity of the Christian can be salvaged by suffering in resistance to the demonic religiosity of modern tyranny. Against the Third Reich, it makes sense to be a

Christian; what makes faith possible in that context is the possibility 'to relive Christ's passion' in powerless vulnerability before others and in service to others.[6] This at least defines what it is to be Christian in a way that the theological pessimism of Barth and the concealed psychologism of Tillich fail to do. But how does this perfectly genuine intensity, of tragedy and witness, relate to the actual world of disenchanted postwar Europe – to Bonhoeffer's church with its chaplaincies to the German armed forces, or Robinson's church, calculating its profits on the Stock Exchange? 'Bonhoeffer's Christianity', writes MacIntyre, 'is, then, intelligible only in one sort of context. Outside that context it lacks precisely any specific differentia from the way of life of sensitive generous liberals.'[7] Worse, 'It clothes ordinary liberal forms of life with the romantic unreality of a catacombic vocabulary.'[8]

Thus the cultural situation of which *Honest to God* is a symptom is that, for the prosaic routinised life of modern Western humanity, there is no obviously plausible language for needs or goals that have to do with more than practical problem solving. But in the problem-solving world, there is an uncomfortable feeling that something has been left out; and this means that religious language is still invoked to dignify a sense of contingency, of the overruling of fate, of fear and fascination in the presence of what isn't understood, the feeling that surely the story of my life has more substance and mystery and meaning than routine language can capture. Once we know that this is what religious language is there for, we can do something with it as adults (MacIntyre published a justly famous article in 1964 under the title, 'Is Understanding a Religion Compatible with Believing It?'). But if we indefinitely defer that recognition, we condemn ourselves to a cultural schism in which religious speech is the property of a self-absorbed minority, borrowed rather uncomfortably for social and psychological purposes somewhat at odds with what that speech is supposed to be talking about. *Honest to God*, MacIntyre is saying, is part of this deferral of truth, and it is, he hints, dangerous precisely because it offers a kind of illicit drama to the user of religious language.

The liberal Christian, vaguely aware that what is being said cannot have real referential content, is encouraged to nurture a self-image as someone living at more 'depth' than others, even living in some obscure way at more risk than others.

I have set out MacIntyre's critique at some length because, almost alone among the first generation of reviews and discussions, it helps the reader now to see some of the cultural appeal of Robinson's book in its context. MacIntyre's verdict overall is unsustainably harsh in regard to Robinson's theological position (and I shall return to this); but he quite rightly pinpoints the consonance between *Honest to God* and a generation of readers for whom the rhetoric of intensity was profoundly attractive. Robinson's reply to MacIntyre does not do a great deal to clarify the difficulties, and rather suggests that he has not taken the point about rhetoric. We read that the real issue between believer and unbeliever is 'whether one can speak of ultimate reality at all and . . . what character this reality has'; and this is given a bit more specificity when Robinson rephrases it in terms of whether 'Jesus' relationship to the reality he could only address as "Abba! Father!" is veridical or not' and 'whether the constitution of the universe [is] such that it justifies' trust like that of Jesus.[9] But this leads to MacIntyre's anxiety about whether this is just claiming for the religious believer a more profound experience of the same environmental data. The danger is that faith becomes a claim to seriousness, the effect of this being to foreclose any debate about discerning between kinds of seriousness, their sustainability or utility or communicability. Faith must surely be more than just an assertion that the believer is more morally interesting than the unbeliever.

The problem in *Honest to God* has a lot to do with a somewhat uncritical use of Tillich, for whom the quality of unconditional self-commitment is repeatedly made the focus of reflection. Discussing Tillich, Robinson says that what makes a statement theological is the degree to which it deals with issues around the ultimate significance of our lives.[10] Robinson clearly agrees to a large extent, but it is again not too clear whether any intensity at all will do or whether it needs to be an intensity directed toward 'the personal'. And in the pages that follow this bold redefinition of theology, Robinson is anxious to put some distance between himself and the Feuerbachian notion that language about God is always and only disguised language about humanity; love, intense personal attention, discloses what is fundamental in the universe but doesn't simply *constitute* it.[11] I think he wants to say that love is fundamental because of the character of 'being itself' – and he is prepared, as in the chapter on Jesus that follows, to speak of some sort of revelation of this, some kind of transparency to what is most ontologically basic, in the life of Christ. Yet there is obvious difficulty in explaining why a sense of the supreme significance of interpersonal attention and respect requires any statement about the universe as such, let alone being as such, whatever.

Both Tillich and Robinson are, of course, battling against what they see as a false and trivialising account of what theology is: it cannot be that theology is simply a set of speculations about a putative member of the class of things that there happen to be.[12] A good many reviewers, with varying degrees of exasperation, pointed out that classical theology repeatedly denied that God was a member of any class whatsoever; the God of the *Summa*, the *Institutes*, or indeed, as David Jenkins noted, the Byzantine Liturgy is anything but a putative individual alongside others.[13] But what Tillich and Robinson are pointing us to is a situation in which theological method has become stale, if not corrupted. If God is indeed what the patristic and scholastic tradition insists God is, that is, the pure act of being, the life beyond categorisation or definition that sustains all particular forms of determinate existence in the coherence of a universe, then theology certainly shouldn't be reduced to a kind of science fiction, dealing with the imagined life of some individual outside the 'normal' boundaries of experience. However, that is how theology regularly degenerates; and when Nietzsche spoke of theological discourse as simply a habit of talking about unreal causes and unreal outcomes, he identified once and for all the risk for theology of becoming just such a fictional discourse, breeding contempt for the real – a 'conspiracy against life'.

What could save theology from such a charge? Only a renewed sense that theological language is a difficult, always incomplete, corruptible, but unavoidable enterprise, pressed into existence by the particular character of what God is perceived as doing, by the sense of a givenness or gratuity bearing on the human situation in such a way that a difference is made that demands new words and concepts. Now this is not, by a very long way, the idiom of *Honest to God*: one of the most startling absences in the book as a whole is surely its reluctance to speak of God as active in any way analogous to the way the word is normally used. It is particularly notable that the chapter on 'Worldly Holiness' discusses prayer in terms quite divorced from any consideration that God might act on the praying person; prayer is, once again, a level of intensity within the ordinary business of interpersonal communication ('I am really praying for people, agonising with God for them, precisely *as* I meet them and really give my soul to them').[14]

But what is significant is the background poverty of thinking about both theology and prayer that provokes Robinson's impatience with traditional form and language in either. It is as if there is no currency for any idea that theology might exist because of the surprising new availability of kinds of prayer in the Christian community; or that there is a narrative of divine action that gives shape to our own action and our praying. To be very specific, the centrality of the doctrine of God as Trinity is nowhere to be found; with the result that the Christology is in fact remarkably abstract. Jesus gives insight into God at work, decisive insight; but it is not clear in what sense he enables a new form of relation to the source of divinity. Despite the tantalising phrase in Robinson's reply to MacIntyre about whether Jesus' relation to God as Father is 'veridical', nothing is explored in this connection that would quite bring out why the eternal intimacy and reciprocity between the source of Godhead and the outflowing of the Godhead, the Father and the Son, should be a cardinally important way of 'holding' what it is that happens in prayer. But my point is that Robinson writes as though such a question were wholly unfamiliar. He doesn't polemicise against this sort of language; indeed, he barely mentions trinitarian doctrine. His targets in 'traditional' theology are both cruder and vaguer. And unfortunately what this implies is that the bulk of the theology Robinson is regularly thinking of is crude and vague, a discourse that appears to be descriptive of a supraworldly agent.

Looking back, it is plain that the postwar period was not nearly such a wilderness from the point of view of robust doctrinal exposition and exploration as this might suggest. Gregory Dix, Austin Farrer and Eric Mascall had all produced work that represented an amazingly creative reworking of classical themes. Dix's *Shape of the Liturgy* offers, in the course of an encyclopedic essay on liturgical development, what is actually a very comprehensive theology of Trinity and incarnation, and the restoration of human personhood and human community in the Eucharist. We might recall his description of the *homo eucharisticus* who is raised up by grace to set against the *homo economicus*, or the consumer in the Mass who is presupposed by the working practices and the advertising culture of modernity.

Farrer had at almost the same time been completing a monumental discussion of theological metaphysics and went on in the postwar period to elaborate (and endlessly revise) his thesis about will as the fundamental analogy for understanding what might be involved in ascribing personal being to God.[15] His brief essays on doctrinal themes are invariably both original and traditional.

In 1946, Mascall, already enjoying a deserved reputation as an expositor of French Thomism, produced a book of doctrinal synthesis, *Christ, the Christian and the Church*, which spells out a coherent and immensely lively dogmatics focused on a rigorous trinitarian and Christological schema and giving exemplary weight to the fact that the New Testament assumes the point of Christ's work to be incorporation into his relation with the Father.[16]

But if the immediate postwar period witnessed such an explosion of first-class Anglican doctrinal reflection, still fresh and suggestive more than fifty years later, it rather looks as though the 1950s had forgotten why any of this mattered. It is in any case significant that the actual enterprise of dogmatics, to use the normal and somewhat forbidding term, was not part of the English university curriculum in theology for the most part. Dix was not a conventional academic theologian; Farrer was professionally a philosopher; Mascall's teaching in the 1950s was likewise primarily philosophical. It could reasonably be said that, despite the extraordinary character of the work that appeared in the mid-forties, there was practically no community of intellectual discourse that allowed the insights of these writers to be discussed and refined. British university theology outside Scotland remained dominated by biblical studies, patristics and 'philosophical theology'; no shortage there of materials for doctrinal work, but such work would have had to be done – from the academic point of view – informally. Add to this the cultural situation of the Church of England in the 1950s, with its renewed institutional confidence, its mildly anti-intellectual leadership, and its half-conscious complicity in the 'end of ideology' mood in the wider intellectual climate, and it is not surprising that the theological attempt to define a place to stand within a narrative of divine action was not high on the corporate Anglican agenda.

In a sense this confirms MacIntyre's point by another route. Anglican, especially Anglo-Catholic, theology had to a degree flourished in an environment of political and cultural crisis – the 1930s and early 1940s. It had mattered intensely as a political thing what models of human nature were to prevail; and the war had, in the eyes of many, once again exposed the emptiness of intellectual modernity and social optimism. Some serious Anglican thinkers at least flirted with Barth, the foremost example probably being Donald MacKinnon. In crisis, the need is for resources to resist. Robinson could have found something of a crisis theology on his doorstep as a young theologian, however different its idiom is from Bonhoeffer. But the general anti-ideological tone of the 1950s was hardly calculated to preserve any sense of why and how these issues had been important; and Robinson was, paradoxically, very much a child of the 1950s in his intellectual style at this point.

Hence the curious tone of nervous jocularity in discussing the theological tradition. No one remembers why doctrines once had a force other than tamely descriptive; the pressure to clarify theological anthropology in unabashed dependence on grace is largely absent. Thus the nuance and qualification, the considerable subtlety of a book like Mascall's on Christology and the Church simply does not register. The motivation for dogmatic excitement, both spiritual and cultural, has become obscure. You could sum up the problem by saying that the good has become obvious in a postideological situation. In such a situation, the question of what distinguishes a believer from an unbeliever is quite hard to answer except in terms of intensity: the believer has no different conception of the good, but does have a more profoundly engaged relation to it, seeing it 'at depth', to use Robinson's favourite metaphor.

Let me try to put this a little differently. The Church of England in the 1950s was mostly unaware of any elements of brooding crisis in its environment – and it can hardly be blamed, given the measurable signs of stability and success. But because this lessened any pressure to define clearly the rationale of its distinctive existence as church, there was actually not very much of what could strictly be called theology. By the beginning of the 1960s, however, the complacent sense of not having to justify oneself was under heavy challenge as the society overall moved toward a more comprehensive consumerisation. When the marketplace increasingly dominates, providers of services need to know what they're about. Less starkly, it is clear enough from Robinson and others that the lack of self-critical awareness in the institutional church in England was becoming an embarrassment, even a scandal. Hence the passionate desire to reclothe Christian commitment with the dignity of risk, depth, or whatever. But the difficulty that *Honest to God* makes plain is that, without some account of how exactly the narrative of God's action discerned by faith questions and reshapes the self's imagining of itself, the distinctive mark of faith will always be in danger of becoming no more than its own asserted human depth, sincerity or seriousness.

This is not necessarily to say that only a conscious recovery of the classical confessional tradition can avoid such a trap, with its high risk of turning theology into a self-dramatising exercise. There are radical alternatives (and Robinson himself famously said in the preface to *Honest to God* that he expected it to be seen in retrospect as not radical enough). In the same year that Robinson's book was published, Werner and Lotte Pelz, refugees from central Europe and already authors of a highly original and searching essay on the prophets, 'True Deceivers', published *God Is No More* – the title being, characteristically, an allusion to William Blake ('Thou art a Man; God is no more').[17] Compared with *Honest to God*, its impact was minimal, partly because it was so densely written, partly because its authors were appreciably less well known than Robinson (though Werner Pelz had worked for some of his life as an Anglican priest). It is a very hard book to classify; the authors deliberately do not set out to redefine the doctrinal tradition, to take sides on issues of biblical historicity, or to propose a programme for the reform of the Church. They are ironically detached about all such issues – even about the issue of whether one should or should not say that God 'exists'; what remains is the *hope* expressed in the words of Jesus, the hope he called 'God', but which we must learn to call whatever we can (including perhaps 'God').[18] His hope is in the strictest sense incredible and imposs-ible: it is that human beings will become capable of living without self-justification, and thus become free for forgiveness because they are focused on the neighbour, not on the self that cries out to be told that it is good. 'The words of Jesus ask us to jump over our shadow or, more correctly, to forget it . . . [O]nly in a friend – not in a shadow, however exalted the name we give it – shall we meet the unexpected, the imponderable that astonishes us and recreates us.'[19] The neighbour must become friend and the friend becomes the only possible concrete manifestation of God. In such a relation, we are not promised harmony and fulfilment, because it must be an adult and a complex matter for people who are equally on the way to something always still to be achieved; it is not about 'peace as the world understands it', but about engaging with the solidity of the neighbour quite apart from the neighbour's ability to fulfil my expectations for being made to feel safe or good.[20]

Jesus is 'unforgivable' for three reasons: He does not give us a 'law', but himself; he relativises or diminishes all that I think of as my achievement; and he fails, he dies, as if his hope is, after all, nonsense. The paradox is that only because of Jesus can we become free to forgive Jesus, to let him live (or make him live?). If we can receive him, not a law or a doctrine, if we can forget the problem of our achievement, if we can understand that there is no final failure so long as witness is given to the hope expressed (incarnated?) once and for all in Jesus, we forgive and are forgiven and become a means of life to one another.[21]

Such a summary gives little sense of the eloquence and freshness of the Pelzes' remarkable book; but it may at least suggest some of the differences between this work and *Honest to God*. The Pelzes share Robinson's move toward identifying the service of God and the presence of God with relation to the neighbour; but the pivotal point is not the intensity of feeling toward the neighbour but the discovery of how the search to justify the self becomes irrelevant in attention to the human other. And the significance of Jesus has little to do, in the Pelzes' book, with his transparency to a universally present love at the root of the universe's existence, but rather with his 'transcendence' of the questions we ask and with the fact that his words are 'never grasped, understood, fulfilled'.[22] Christian identity for the Pelzes seems both more and less 'secular' than for Robinson: they have no particular anxieties about reshaping a metaphysical idiom for God, and the book is a long way from anything like an ecclesiastical agenda (though it has some powerfully suggestive thoughts on the meaning of the Eucharist).

But the governing images are clearly marked by the sense of being addressed, interrupted, by the words of Jesus, and summoned to a reimagining of yourself. Jesus makes something possible. It is always unachieved as soon as we start to find words for it or reflect on our performances in relation to it. But there is a pervasive awareness of some sort of gratuity presented to us.

Robinson is far more consciously working within a framework of liturgy and doctrine, even while arguing for drastic reinterpretation. Yet, as noted earlier, there is relatively little sense of an agency beyond the sum of human agencies, and thus of a gift bestowed. The chapter on 'The New Morality' in *Honest to God* seems to suggest that there remains a right answer to ethical dilemmas, and that this is provided by 'love', which 'has a built-in moral compass, enabling it to "home" intuitively upon the deepest need of the other'.[23] This contrasts sharply with the Pelzes' concern with letting go of justification (even by love) and their awareness of the labour of creating friendship in the response to the neighbour and of the ineradicability of some kinds of enmity. The surface of the two arguments has something in common; deeper down, there are very different agendas at work, that of the Pelzes perhaps more typically European in its sense of the tragic and its Lutheran passions about justification.

I am not trying to say that *God Is No More* is right and *Honest to God* wrong, but only to note one example of restoring some substance to the distinction of believer from unbeliever without simply appealing to the believer's superior moral intensity. The Pelzes may sound as if that is what they are interested in, but the whole discussion of justification gives content to the intensity in a way hard to discern in Robinson and his mentor Tillich. Yet, as I have intimated, content may also be restored by some sort of reclaiming of the doctrinal tradition itself. In the 1960s, there was little sign of this; and up to the later 1970s it remained true that the consensus of Anglican academic theology was not too sympathetic to the idea that credal formulations might be a fruitful way into discussing the crises of modernity. The 1976 report of the Doctrine Commission of the Church of England, *Christian Believing*, probably represented the high-water mark of this detachment from doctrinal tradition; much of it was a long way from Robinson's concerns, and it certainly did not echo the Tillichian and Bultmannian rhetoric of authenticity. But it can be read as one of the outcomes of the processes of which *Honest to God* was such a significant part, the processes of forgetting that the language of classical doctrine originated in the sense of a gift of transformation or conversion.

Several things were stirring by 1976 that would change the landscape further. The enormous new interest in the history of Christian spirituality, the popularity of writers like Thomas Merton, and the beginnings of a new interest in the Christian East made the 1960s' models of 'worldly holiness' look a little thin. In a way wholly typical of his intellectual generosity and spiritual sensitivity, Robinson himself, in his *Exploration into God*,[24] had already begun to think through some of these issues (it is intriguing that he made such use of the Romanian novelist Petru Dumitriu in this work; Dumitriu was to publish some years later a personal account of his return to a rather unconventional Christian faith, showing a complex relationship to the Eastern Orthodox heritage of his country).

But there was also a rapidly growing interest in the theology of Continental Europe: English translations of Bultmann and Bonhoeffer no longer satisfied younger theologians looking for a fuller understanding of how the history of the mid-century had impacted European theology. The work of Jürgen Moltmann was being translated by 1970 and had immense impact. By the late 1970s, more theologians were turning back to Barth for inspiration. In the whole of this process, the issues of Christian anthropology and the doctrine of God as Trinity were coming more and more into the centre of intellectual concern. By the early 1980s, *Honest to God* seemed a museum piece; the philosophical and doctrinal idioms regarded by Robinson and many of his generation as speculative indulgences had become keystones in all kinds of ambitious new constructions.

It would make a tidy and satisfying tale if we could simply say that *Honest to God* was a transient phenomenon at a time of rapid change and intellectual deracination in the Church. It certainly breathes a cultural optimism very much of its day and a psychological *naïveté* in regard to its moral concerns. The wonderful question put into the mouth of a 1960s' cartoon character (Charlie Brown in *Peanuts*), 'How can I be wrong if I'm so sincere?' sums up an entire cultural moment in a way that can't easily be improved on. But the work's significance cannot be dismissed so swiftly and patronisingly. The very unclarity about the doctrine of God that some reviewers (not least Thomists like Mascall and Herbert McCabe) deplored is actually deeply instructive. Robinson was emphatically right to observe that, whatever theologians might say, a huge amount of both popular and sermonic talk about God did indeed treat God as a member of the class of things that there are in the universe; and some of the enthusiastic retrieval by theologians in the 1980s and 1990s of versions of the dogmatic tradition is far less sensitive than Robinson to this problem (look, for example, at some of the really remarkable assertions about gendered language for God sometimes advanced by would-be traditionalists).

One of the major challenges to any restatement or defence of the classical credal theology is the task of tracing the divine action in revelatory history without reinstating a fundamentally mythological idiom for speaking of that divine action. The temptation to argue for a 'biblical' theology in which there are no problems in ascribing to God an action that is episodic and temporal, in treating God as, effectively, an agent among other agents in time, has been strong for many, sometimes reinforced by a superficial reading of Barth. *Honest to God* was not mistaken in diagnosing a problem and pointing out the dangers of fairy-tale language. Where I think it is inadequate in its analysis is in supposing that the difficulty comes from new cultural factors. We are told that it has become impossible to believe this or that because of changes in philosophy or science. A more nuanced understanding would note that Christian theology from at least the third century has been aware of the problem and seen it as intrinsic to all attempts to speak of God as active. The late Dominican philosopher Gareth Moore, in his luminous essay on *Believing in God*, reiterates the Thomist principle that creation is not any kind of process: that something comes into being and that God created it amount to the same; the existence of the being is the act of God.[25] This is not a response to new difficulties posed by modernity, but a restatement of venerable principles.

But, venerable as they may be, they are no more currently recognised than in 1963 in the realm of professional and semi-professional theology. Robinson's protests are intelligible, even if, to quote Herbert McCabe, 'the book suffers a good deal from the author's lack of acquaintance with the history of theology.'[26] Reading the book now can still awaken a fresh awareness of the problem: the fact that it is difficult to talk about God and that an unexamined discourse purporting to be about the doings of a super-worldly individual is a dangerous substitute for real theology.

A good deal of what I have been trying to suggest in these pages relates to MacIntyre's challenge to Robinson: Is the language of *Honest to God* essentially secular substance in 'catacombic' rhetoric? Whatever Robinson's purposes, there is some uncomfortable plausibility to the charge, especially in what I believe to be the weakest chapters of the book (on prayer and on ethics). But because he does not have a language capable of saying something about the objectivity of God without suggesting anthropomorphism, because he is not too familiar with the kind of self-critical realism of some of his Thomist reviewers, he has no clear way of distinguishing the active existence of God from what is simply 'at the heart' of the universe. That God is God without respect to the universe's existence is not, for Robinson, easy to state. But I am in little doubt that this is what he would have regarded as a necessary condition of all that he does find to say of God; and his later work bears this out. I don't think that he is in this sense a forerunner of the antirealists of more recent times – Don Cupitt and his followers. My concern is rather that the lack of a robust spiritual contextualising of doctrinal language, a lack entirely explicable in the atmosphere of the theological discussions of the late 1950s and early 1960s, leaves the rhetoric in possession of the field at the expense of content. Donald MacKinnon wrote in 1975 a particularly searching article on Tillich and some of his contemporaries in which he charged Tillich with yielding to the temptation 'of seeing himself in his own eyes as one taking upon himself the most demanding and most frightening tasks, emancipated both by the aims, and indeed by the content, of his enterprise from the discipline of a self-questioning that reaches the very substance of what he is in himself. He is always a Romantic.'[27] This would be an excessively hard judgement on Robinson, whose temperamental unlikeness to Tillich undoubtedly saved him from what MacKinnon sees as a sort of posturing on the edge of the abyss; Robinson remains committed to 'purifying the dialect' of a church that is not composed of a Romantic elite. Yet, when the experiential and spiritual content of doctrine has been distorted or obliterated, where is one to locate the transformation offered by faith except in the vividness of the quality of engagement with the world's tasks? And that will always have the effect of making the believer a kind of moral hero, which sits uncomfortably with any commitment to justification by faith (which is why I signal Werner and Lotte Pelz's book as a pendant to Robinson's).

Few readers may have grasped the technicalities of the book, and judging from the responses collated and discussed by Robert Towler in his study of reactions to *Honest to God*, not all that many read it as commending or endorsing Tillichian heroism.[28] The general tone of the positive reactions is one of relief at being given permission to express dismay or disillusion at the uncritical language of what I have called the semiprofessional theological world. But if we are seeking an explanation for the fantastic success of the book in terms of sales, I suspect part of the answer lies in its rhetoric of depth, sincerity and intensity. However poorly it was understood, the notion of the moral dignity of religious belief communicated itself somehow to the reading public. But it was a belief very loosely anchored indeed to either narrative or community – the two most influential contextual issues in about 80 per cent of dogmatic theology written in English since 1980. Dignity was perceived as attached to personal fervour and integrity. But these were not conceived or assessed with reference to a governing narrative (and it is perhaps in ethics that the greatest damage has been done). Robinson touched a cultural nerve, in a way unparalleled since 1963.

There is another curious and rather paradoxical aspect of the book. It was the last religious book in the United Kingdom to have anything that could remotely be called a mass readership. In that sense, just as Luther is the last of the Rhineland mystics, so Robinson is the last of the mass religious authors. *Honest to God* is in that sense part of the very phenomenon whose decline or decadence prompted its writing. Its popularity reflects a cultural situation in which the affairs of the Church of England in particular could still attract media attention that was not simply anecdotal or prurien – and in which a measure of literacy about the Bible and about religious issues in general might be expected in the educated reading public. But what motivates Robinson is just the sense that this cultural interest is stretched as thinly as it will go, as more and more people find the Church's idiom inaccessible or absurd. If the culture is in any sense to be saved for the Church, the Church must learn to speak in other ways. The effect is, arguably, to let the culture of the early 1960s set the agenda all too firmly. Yet the underlying concern is, again, intelligible, especially given the sense of bereavement felt by a church whose involvement in the public life of the national culture had been recently pretty strong and whose official involvement remained (and remains) very visible.

Honest to God could only have been written by an Anglican at such a moment in history – which tells us much about Anglicanism in its home territory and much about that moment. Perhaps it could only have been written by someone who, like Robinson, had been at the centre of academic and ecclesiastical establishment, yet was blessed with a mind never content with establishment solutions. It is not in the usual sense a 'great book'; its flaws are too evident, and it does not make a coherent and original contribution to its subject matter. Yet it is the book of a great man, a lovable and faithful servant of Christ as many (including myself) will willingly testify. And there is a kind of stature in its 'iconic' (to use an unhappy jargon term) status as crystallising some of the intellectual self-doubt of 1960s' Christianity. I have tried to identify the ways in which it continues to pose utterly necessary questions – by what it says and by what it fails to say – and I am convinced that it will go on bearing fresh readings for a very long time yet. It leaves us above all with the question, MacIntyre's question, of how a language of faith rooted in experiences and expressions of 'extremity' can be rendered in a bourgeois environment without self-serving drama. And if it reminds us of the dangers (for the churches as for everyone else) of an 'end of ideology' intellectual culture, an abdication from the critique of our cultural constructions of the self in public and private relations, it will be salutary reading indeed.

EIGHT

B.F. WESTCOTT (1825–1901)
E.C. HOSKYNS (1884–1937)
WILLIAM TEMPLE (1881–1944) and
JOHN A.T. ROBINSON (1919–1983)

Anglican Approaches to St John's Gospel

ROBERT BROWNING'S DRAMATIC monologue, *A Death in the Desert*, appeared in 1864, one of the remarkable sequence entitled *Dramatis Personae*. It remains one of the most intriguing and complex religious poems of the era: a full study of it would need a chapter to itself, and a formidable comparative exercise drawing in Strauss, Kierkegaard, George Eliot and several other giants of the age. The apostle John is dying, hidden in a cave, attended by a few disciples; he knows that with him will die the last concrete link with the events of Jesus' life, and he reflects on what this will mean for generations ahead. Out of this meditation comes a kind of rationale for the text of his gospel, flowering into something like an entire theory of revelation and religious knowledge.

The first 'blaze' of revelation compels, or should compel, in much the same sense as fire warms. But what it means, how it changes lives, can only be charted with the passage of time. Those who were closest to Jesus also betrayed and forsook him, yet in a

few years' time new converts who had never met him in the flesh
embrace martyrdom for his sake without hesitation. The direct
apprehension of revelation is also, paradoxically, vulnerable to the
direct threat of 'a torchlight and a noise, /The sudden Roman
faces, violent hands'; those who have grown into some fullness of
understanding love are stronger. Yet for them the temptation is
still there; not this time in the immediate physical threat, but in
the uncritical assumption that growing in understanding involves
leaving behind the concrete beginning. Why not, as understanding
grows, accept that what once was thought revealed is actually a
discovery of what is already within? The story of the gospel
becomes the *occasion* for realising that we already possess the truth
delivered.

> 'Tis mere projection from man's inmost mind,
> And, what he loves, thus falls reflected back,
> Becomes accounted somewhat out of him;
> He throws it up in air, it drops down earth's,
> With shape, name, story added, man's old way.

The answer is laboured but comprehensive. To apprehend God is
to be aware of power, will and love together. We begin with
awareness of a power more fundamental than the forces of nature;
but if we interpret this power as negating will in us or as irreconci-
lable with the idea of will in God, we arrive at a static and sterile
position, denying what is basic in our own humanity, which is
precisely the combination of power and reflective freedom. So too
with love: to deny eternal love as the basis of both power and will
(because love is something we think we know and practise in our
human relations) is to frustrate our own humanity, which needs
a constantly increasing consciousness of being loved and being
equipped to love. If there is no love beyond the human capacity,
humanity is frozen. The very dynamism of humanity's growth
requires us to look beyond humanity as the measure of everything,
and thus to reject the idea that what causes us to grow must be

projection. But – and here is the relevance of this to the gospel – humanity learns what it itself is in the process of history and in no other way. And to understand more deeply what is actually trans-acted in the concrete happening of the world is constantly the exercise that makes us human, even though that understanding is by trial and error.

So the setting out of an historical story becomes indispensable to the human quest for truth. This is the narrative of how we are loved, recorded by an eyewitness whose own history of growth has 'opened' the facts more and more to what they signify. 'What first were guessed as points, I now knew stars': the gospel isolates events rather like looking through the wrong end of a telescope to give distance and perspective to otherwise confused details. The reader must

> . . . stand before that fact, that Life and Death,
> Stay there at gaze, till it dispart, dispread,
> As though a star should open out, all sides,
> And grow the world on you, as it is my world.

And so, as the coda to the poem, written in the voice of an early Christian named Pamphylax, explains, each human person's growth is a 'filling-up' with the life of Christ, the power and will and love which allows each to be himself or herself: Christ as 'groom for each bride'. In reading the gospel, we find ourselves as we could not do for ourselves; to recognise Christ as God is to learn to see him as in this sense the fulfilment of each of us, completing who we are. 'Can a mere man do this?'

I have dealt at some length with this very complex poem because it is referred to as a kind of benchmark by all four of the Anglican authors I want to examine in the rest of this chapter. If there is any kind of apostolic succession in Anglican commentary it is provided in part by the reflections of this unusual Nonconformist poet, who is quoted by all of them in their Johannine work. I shall be looking briefly at Bishop Westcott's commentary on the English text, at E.C. Hoskyns' uncompleted work, edited by Noel Davey, William Temple's *Readings in St John's Gospel* and John A.T. Robinson's *Priority of John* – uncomfortably aware that each requires a full study in its own right, but seeking to chart one strand in interpretation which we shan't understand without bearing in mind Browning's poem; for it is Browning who seems to be the first to use the Fourth Gospel as a springboard for detailed reflection on history and faith in the mode that all these authors, in one way or another, take for granted.

First, to Westcott. I use his earlier commentary on the English text, since this is the one that had more impact on the general theological mind of British and especially Anglican Christianity, although his larger commentary on the Greek is where the New Testament scholar will more readily turn.[1] Westcott's introduction offers an analysis of the movement of the whole text in terms of a double cycle of narrative and discourse – Christ's self-revelation to the world (chapters 1–12) and his self-revelation to the disciples (chapters 13–21), both culminating in definitive episodes of controversy and conflict. Throughout the whole, Westcott suggests, the narrative is shaped by three paired themes: truth and witness, light and glory, judgement and life. The entire gospel sets out the enactment of these themes as they are defined in the teaching and the conflict narrated. Witness – God's witness to Christ above all – is effective in terms of the breaking in of light, and what is then visible is truth as glory. But this glory is visible only to those who pass through judgement, who are in some sense separated from the error of the world. To pass through judgement is identical with being where Christ is; it is both present and future, 'self-fulfilled' (p. xlix) but still enacted by God. 'The historical execution of judgment, both present and final, is recognised as a work of the Son'; and it is possible historically because of the Word's total identification with human nature: as truly, not only representatively, human, Christ displays what it is that all are judged by, the humanity that exists in unbroken relation with the Father, even through the conditions of weakness and vulnerability and death.

Every stage in Christ's self-revelation is thus a specific call for decision for or against his humanity, his actual particular flesh and blood. 'St John lays open the course of the original conflict which is the pattern of all conflicts to the end of time.'[2]

Thus Westcott seems to be suggesting that if we foreground the theme of judgement in the gospel, judgement that is rooted in the exemplary humanity of Jesus, we cannot dehistoricise the theology of the gospel without dissolving its logic. Because this is a specific human life, lived at this moment in these geographical locations, it can serve as a point of judgement; divorced from this, the unique recognition of the action of God inseparably involved in our relations with a particular person becomes impossible. God's act of judgement would have to be reconceived as eschatologically deferred and therefore presently uncertain. The narrative of the gospel assumes that judgement is passed *now*, definitively. This does not mean that an ecclesial power can now determine some-one's eternal fate; that is not the framework in which the evangelist operates. It is simply that, as a matter of fact (whether or not it is discernible to anyone), reaction to Jesus defines life and death.

Westcott is thus fairly flexible about historical detail, particularly in respect of the discourses of the gospel. All records of facts are records of 'representative details';[3] words used to summarise a discourse may leave us not much the wiser about what was said on a specific occasion. The point of the record is to show how judgement is enacted in particulars, even where the particulars are in *some* degree selective or imaginatively ordered. Yet Westcott is careful to argue also that even in the Farewell Discourses we can discern a historically convincing movement of thought. The record is neither photographically exact nor freely composed. Its core must be an actual encounter or dialogue, otherwise the fundamental point about judgement would fall.

Something of Browning's concerns will already have become visible. Westcott, who greatly admired Browning, borrows else-where the image of 'standing at gaze' when we look at the incidents of the gospel record. And that there are things that can be learned only as time unfolds the relation with Jesus is clearly to the fore in much of Westcott's exegesis. Perhaps some of the clearest echoes of, especially, the coda to Browning's poem appear in Westcott's pages on the characters of the gospel, where, with a finely imaginative hand, he illustrates how encounter with Jesus displays and completes a character in the narrative, and how in particular the words ascribed to the disciples define the stages and varieties of faith. Reflecting on John 4:8 and on the various sayings associated with Thomas, Westcott says, 'Philip believed without confidence, Thomas believed without hope';[4] he shows how the typical failures or weaknesses of faith represented here are still authentically faithful, since they are open to the completion given in Christ's response to them. Westcott uses the psychological vividness of these and other exchanges as an argument for the direct eyewitness basis of the narrative, in a way which later scholars may find naïve. But the point in Westcott's exegesis is that the theological centre remains a conviction that the distinctive character of the revelation of Christ is found in the enactment of judgement relative to a concrete human figure and a set of concrete human relations with that figure.

Thus the gospel both affirms the particularity of the mode of Christ's revelation and warns against assuming that this particularity can be reduced to a simple telling of the story as an exact record of past events. Browning, remember, notes the ambiguity of 'first-generation' or eyewitness faith: it remains vulnerable to external threat so long as the concrete personal presence has not been apprehended as the soul's 'bride'. The complexities of this are explored a good deal further in E.C. Hoskyns' torso of a commentary, published in 1940.[5] Noel Davey, introducing the work, which he had laboured to complete after Hoskyns' death, notes what many reviewers failed to pick up – that Hoskyns had intended the commentary to be modelled on Barth's *Romans*, which he had translated. His working methods changed significantly during the time he was working on the Barth translation, and one of the many reasons for the non-completion of the

Johannine study was his attempt to recast all his previous drafts in a form similar to that of the Romans commentary. This recasting was only taken as far as chapter 7 at the time of his death; the revised style of the commentary on the earlier chapters is tantalising evidence of what could have been.[6]

Hoskyns' introductory material is immensely compressed and abstract, in his usual mode, even with Davey's skilful editing (especially of the seventh chapter of the introduction, which is mostly his work in its present form). However, there is a clear line of argument overall, indicated early on in his survey of earlier research, where he takes on the 'critical orthodoxy' of German exegesis, which concentrates on the supposedly 'mystical' emphasis in John, and his Hellenistic concern with metaphysical structures. Like Temple, to whom we shall be returning shortly, Hoskyns is very unhappy with 'mystical' as a designation for the gospel (one suspects that contact with Barth had reinforced this): 'The visible, historical Jesus', he writes, 'is the place in history where it is demanded that men should believe',[7] where ultimate divisions are set up between those who believe and those who do not. A reading of the narrative as 'mystical' in the sense of dealing in allegories, stories or images that illustrate truths about the internal structures of belief in God, would be wholly unthinkable in such a perspective. Yet, as for Westcott (whose theology is clearly recalled here, even though Hoskyns' summary of him makes relatively little of the importance of the 'judgement' theme), this cannot be taken to imply that we are dealing with a simple record. Hoskyns, in a powerfully expressed passage, argues that incidents in the Synoptic tradition, above all the Transfiguration and the Agony, are, so to speak, spread through the whole of the gospel; they become the hidden hermeneutical key to the entire narrative, and, as such, cannot be simply narrated as episodes among others. Narrated in this way, they would not appear to us as the clue to the whole.[8]

The life of Jesus in the flesh is '*the place of understanding*',[9] and it would therefore be absurd if the specificities of that life were ignored or distorted by the evangelist. But how do we tell a story in such a way as to uncover the relation of the acts and episodes to a truth that is in no sense the product of an historical process? Hoskyns again echoes Browning's cautions about misreading the fact that we learn historically as if it meant that we are constantly coming to points where we can discard the conditions of the process – a kind of triumphalist evolutionism in the theological sphere. If revelation is not a process, but the reception of it is inseparably bound to historical narratives of change and growth, we face a considerable problem. Hoskyns/Davey (for this is dis- cussed in the chapter largely drafted by Davey in its present form) compares this to how we talk about Providence. We cannot *deduce* Providence from analysis of an historical process, because the doc- trine demands that we see God's hand in everything; to speak otherwise is to absorb God's action into the business of human contingencies (Barth on the horizon again), to identify it with successful performances within the world, and thus to shut out from God's sphere what does not conform to such successful performance. Theologising about Providence requires a patient looking at the circumstances of history until their relation to the nature and purposes of God appears – not a 'manipulation' of history to prove a point, with all the selectivity and distortion that entails.[10]

Apply this to the gospel: look at how the gospel treats time itself, its use of past and future and present tenses. Look at the subversion of ordinary tenses in Jesus' 'I am' sayings; or at his own use of the future. 'There is on His lips no casual use of the future tense': he speaks of the future to speak of the absolute consistency of what he always is, or of the manifesting in what is to come of what already is.[11] The appeal to the Spirit in the Fourth Gospel is meant to 'carry' all this – to avoid a futurist eschatology of a crude sort and to clarify that what is to come is the encounter with Jesus, nothing else. The Spirit shows that 'the end' is already Jesus. 'The doctrine of the Holy Spirit is the fourth Evangelist's protection against the imposition of an interpretation upon the history he records.'[12] The Spirit as it were holds the telling of

Jesus' story in such a way that it cannot be absorbed into an historical series, cannot be made part of an evolutionary story. The Spirit possesses this narrative and presents it to us as always contemporary. Yet the point of all this is not to isolate the events of Jesus' life from all of history but to make it possible for us, by encountering *this* portion of history, to see how we may encounter the God of Jesus in all history. Yet we cannot see him everywhere unless we see him first in one unique place: 'that Life and Death' can be seen as '*the* event which bestows upon all events their theological meaning, mediating the love of God and His judgement, eternal life and eternal condemnation'.[13]

So Hoskyns can be read as building upon Westcott's concern with judgement; but also upon Browning's nuanced dealing with the evolutionary difficulty, as we might call it. How do we simultaneously attend to the realities of growth, the impossibility of absorbing faith in Christ by means of a mere record independently of his entering into each of us as our personal completion, and the risks of reducing God to a conclusion in a human story, the end of a human trajectory – and so making God less than God, as both Browning and Hoskyns in their diverse ways see it? Hoskyns does not offer an answer in the abstract, but simply encourages us to read the gospel in this light, assuming that we shall not understand it unless we 'take our stand where the Evangelist stood'[14] – that is, in the perspective given by the Spirit, which holds the narrative before us in its own right or in its own space – perhaps like the optical instrument which Browning's St John describes, which allows confused things to 'Become succinct, distinct, so small, so clear!' And it is in this appeal to standing where the evangelist stands that Hoskyns most clearly echoes the Barth who in introducing his Romans commentary insists that we cannot read Paul unless we assume that he has seen what we long to see.

Of these four authors, William Temple is the one who has impacted most powerfully on the popular religious mind. His *Readings*[15] formed the staple of several generations of Anglican clergy and laypeople (and of course many beyond the Anglican frontier), and the influence of the book has still not entirely waned. It manages to be both more and less than a commentary in the normal sense: it offers a variety of observations on specific questions of exegesis, but is more of a protracted meditation on the text, of the kind that kindles intelligent devotion. Like my other examples, Temple quotes Browning's poem as 'the most penetrating interpretation of St John that exists in the English language' (and indeed his biography witnesses to his early and lasting fondness for Browning's oeuvre in general); and like Westcott and Hoskyns, he is best read as reacting strongly against the tendency to make the evangelist a 'mystic'. The publication of the first volume antedates Hoskyns' work by a year, and Hoskyns will have been too far advanced in his last illness to have taken notice of Temple; but there are some striking convergences, suggesting very strongly a twin derivation from themes in Westcott.

'It is . . . vital to St John's purpose that the events which he records should be actual events', he writes;[16] but, with his predecessors, he does not wish to bind the credibility of the text too closely to exact reportage, especially in respect of the discourses. He takes up in a more direct way than the others, the 'moral' question of whether the self-assertive note of so much of Jesus' teaching in the Fourth Gospel compromises our taking it seriously – very much a mid-twentieth-century sort of anxiety, though not one on which Hoskyns spends much time – and responds that everything depends on whether you believe that what Jesus says of himself is true (very much a mid-twentieth-century answer, if you think of some of C.S. Lewis's apologetic from the same era). But he is content to allow a fair measure of the evangelist's own liberty at work in the creation of the discourses as they stand, and goes so far as to say that it is the same Jesus who speaks 'whether in the flesh or in the experience of His beloved disciple',[17] a concession which in those bare terms may be thought to go rather further than the rest of the introduction implies. But he qualifies this at once by noting that even when a saying may not be exact reportage, or any kind of reportage, its reliability is established by its present and effectual truth: what Jesus is represented as speaking *about* happens or has happened. So it is with 'I will not leave you desolate'; the important fact is that we are *not* left desolate.[18]

The polemic against 'mysticism' is very clearly expressed, on the understanding (which might well be challenged, of course) that the mystical is essentially about *unmediated* knowledge of the divine. It is in this context that Temple utters what may be his most quoted aphorism, that 'Christianity is the most materialistic of all great religions'.[19] Like Hoskyns, he wants to say that the identification of certain elements in the world and its history as supremely significant of God must be inseparably bound up with a theology that proclaims the entire spatio-temporal order as potentially significant of God. Hence his insistence on the *sacramental* as the governing theme in John's Gospel, in a way which has something in common with Westcott's observations on John 6 ('through the Incarnation, the relations between things outward and inward, things seen and unseen, are revealed to us as real and eternal, and not superficial and transitory'[20]). The evangelist is careful not to use the language of 'Spirit' in any way that might detract from the specificity of relation with the material history of Jesus, which is why he stresses so firmly the 'materialistic' elements in the eucharistic discourse of chapter 6. We cannot receive Christ either by contemplating abstract religious ideals or even by 'recollection of such scenes from His life as we prefer to contemplate'.[21] We encounter Jesus in the materiality of the sacrament; yet this is not a magical transaction in which one bit of material stuff is miraculously transferred from one location to another. It is to say that where this action takes place, the eating of bread and wine in Jesus' name and power, heaven is present, encounter occurs. The whole pattern is close to Westcott's discussion; but it can profitably be looked at in connection with Hoskyns' theology of the Spirit as well.

The eucharistic character of the discourse in chapter 6 remains controversial in recent exegesis; but Temple's argument is not so much about eucharistic theology on its own as about the whole issue of *mediation* in the knowledge of God. Yes, there is awareness of God in the very fact of our being made in the divine image; but the mind which takes itself for its own object in seeking clues about the divine nature will fail and fail dangerously, because of the mental and spiritual distortion imposed by sin. We need mediation and therefore imagery; without the revelation of the true image, our imagery will be idolatry.[22] And this is how personal being works: revelation is not the delivery of truths detached from the medium of their giving, but personal presence acting on personal intelligence – and thus, in our world as it actually is, acting through historical and material fact. 'The Incarnation is not a condescension to our infirmities . . . It is the only way in which divine truth can be expressed.'[23]

This is only the briefest of summaries of some of Temple's leading themes. In one sense, he contributes little, if anything, that is new to the tradition of reading I have been tracing; but his aphoristic clarity and the accessibility of his reflection, coloured by vivid language, personal anecdote and manifest felt engagement with the text, made the tradition available to many who would certainly not have opened Hoskyns. And the sacramentalist account of history, the stress on mediated knowledge and thus on narrative and practice, could well be taken as a statement of the theological consensus of the mid-twentieth century in the Anglican world – a little bolder and more explicit than Westcott on sacramentality, a little less ferocious about definitive judgement and the discontinuity of God with human process than Hoskyns (Barth was beginning, but only beginning, to make an impact on most British theologians of the period, and Temple was a latecomer to appreciation of the genius of Bonn and Basel), yet recognisably crystallising a view whose roots are in both the high Victorian synthesis of history and theology represented by Browning and in an older and very broadly Christian Platonist model of the right use of material signs.

And part of the interest of John Robinson's posthumously

published work on *The Priority of John*[24] is that it can be read as defence of just this Anglican and Browningite consensus against the ever-colder blasts of more recent Johannine scholarship. Although the main burden of the book is to establish the case for an early date for the Fourth Gospel, there is a wealth of reflection here on some of the themes we have been examining (not to mention the obligatory references to Browning). In order to argue that the teaching of John's Jesus is not different *toto caelo* from that of the Synoptic Jesus, Robinson has to enter the lists with those who read John in a gnosticising fashion, and thus to address some of the now familiar issues about history and faith. Robinson notes that the discourses and the narrative are far more closely integrated than the summaries of some scholars would suggest and that they can on occasion correspond to known homiletic patterns in first-century synagogue teaching;[25] protracted meditative styles of spoken teaching are not nearly as unlikely as might be supposed, and we must not leap to sceptical conclusions too rapidly. The supposedly 'mystical' idiom must be thought about carefully; we cannot take for granted that mystical and apocalyptic rhetoric could not co-exist (rather the contrary now that we have begun to digest Qumran), and this again does not furnish a clear ground for marking off the Johannine Jesus' teaching as a late and hybrid construct.[26] What John's Jesus speaks of is not, despite all efforts to make it so, a prescription for internalised piety oriented to self-discovery.[27] The commitment to concrete *koinonia* is 'stronger than that of any other New Testament writer, except . . . Paul',[28] and it is a distortion to represent Johannine *agape* as more directed to fellow-believers than to the world.[29]

But some of Robinson's most interesting proposals come in his final chapter on the Person of Christ. The chapter begins by affirming robustly that John has no interest in discarding or demeaning the flesh, but only in 'allowing it to become diaphanous to spirit'.[30] This is further developed in terms of three ways of seeing the historical processes described – from the outside, 'from the outside in' (tracing the actual steps in understanding as they are enacted by the characters), and 'from the inside out', from the perspective of those who have come to stand at the centre of it all, where the Son himself stands. From this last perspective, a good deal of freedom can be allowed in narrating events or discourses, because the focal meanings are clear. And all these are distinguished from a position characterised as 'seeing simply *on the inside*' – an esoteric vision which can wholly dispense with the details of concrete narrative and material communication.[31]

It leads Robinson finally to some intriguing speculation about the inner life of Jesus, which he rightly calls the last taboo of New Testament studies.[32] A lengthy discussion here concludes by assimilating the 'I' of Jesus' self-designating statements to the 'I' of some sorts of Eastern mysticism. The speaker is speaking, in such statements, neither as a simple empirical human subject, nor as a subject from another world, but as one who has realised a fundamental unity with the depth of all reality. We should not, therefore, reject the historicity of the 'I-sayings' as if they could only be read (as they have always been by traditionally orthodox exegetes) as evidence for consciousness of pre-existence. Rather they designate a humanity which has received the fullness of relationship with God which God purposes for all humanity – a purpose which, because it is eternal in God's mind, can in some sense be regarded as a pre-existent reality.

To be honest, I find this section of Robinson's discussion probably the weakest. He is (as elsewhere) awkward in his handling of the traditional categories of Chalcedonian and post-Chalcedonian Christology, making the common mistake of treating the idea of an 'anhypostatic' humanity in Jesus as if it meant some incompleteness, psychological or metaphysical, in his human individuality. It is also clear that anything like a full-blown trinitarian theology becomes very hard to extract from Robinson's scheme. It is noticeable that Hoskyns' concentration on the Spirit is wholly absent from the theological discussion of the last chapters, and he seems content with the odd doctrine of Schoonenberg[33] that the Logos has no 'personal' subsistence prior to the birth of Jesus. But I think that this focuses the area in which Robinson, despite the considerable common ground with the other writers we have been looking at, misses a central theme in this exegetical tradition – a theme which I can best characterise as that of revelatory and creative judgement.

The drift of Robinson's argument is that Jesus represents that which is potentially there in all human beings; that he realises the fulfilled consciousness of union with the source of all things as Father to which all humanity is summoned – and that in so doing he also embodies as fully as possible the divine will and purpose and nature. All of this is of course part of the earlier readings we have looked at, and of the mainstream of exegesis behind it. But the three earlier interpreters all give some prominence (Westcott and Hoskyns most of all) to the Johannine theme of self-discovery by way of confrontation with Jesus, a theme which is adumbrated so distinctively in the coda to Browning's poem:

'If Christ, as thou affirmest, be of men
Mere man, the first and best but nothing more, –
    Account Him, for reward of what He was,
        Now and for ever, wretchedest of all.
    For see; Himself conceived of life as love,
        Conceived of love as what must enter in,
Fill up, make one with His each soul He loved:
Thus much for man's joy, all men's joy for Him.
Well, He is gone, thou sayest, to fit reward.
    But by this time are many souls set free,
        And very many still retained alive:
Nay, should His coming be delayed awhile,
Say, ten years longer (twelve years, some compute)
    See if, for every finger of thy hands,
There be not found, that day the world shall end,
Hundreds of souls, each holding by Christ's word
    That He will grow incorporate with all,
With me as Pamphylax, with him as John,

Groom for each bride! Can a mere man do this?
Yet Christ saith, this He lived and died to do.
Call Christ, then, the illimitable God,
Or lost!'

If there is any conclusion to be drawn from this sketchy survey
of Anglican exegesis, it is perhaps this: If historical mediation is
essential to a distinctively Christian account of the knowledge of
God, that history must be seen as always and irreducibly other to
us. There is a dimension of the knowledge of God in Christ that
is never capable of being absorbed into self-recognition only. We
are not yet ourselves in the event of self-recognition if that is only
a perception of what humanity is capable of. As Westcott, Hoskyns
and Temple all observed, in their very diverse idioms, our selfhood
is made real in the face of the other – a divine other whose divine
otherness is identical in this world with the historical, material
givenness of a particular life and death. The tough paradox of
Johannine faith is that, for the purposes of our growth into life,
the transcendent reality which does not and cannot occupy a shared
space with us is only accessible and functional as another portion
of the world, a fleshly human life. The difficulty of faith is not
simply to realise in ourselves a capacity long since given but long
since overgrown. It is to apprehend the 'place' in the historical
world occupied by this human life as a place where in principle
any mortal can stand – or perhaps to apprehend the place where any
mortal stands as capable of being identical with the place of Jesus.
For that apprehension to happen, the life set before us must so be
characterised by the self-forgetting of love that it is met as presenting us with no impassable boundaries; and it must so challenge
us as to where we wish to be, on which side of certain lines, that
our account of ourselves must change as a result. This, I think, is
implicit in what Hoskyns argues about the role of the Spirit in
'holding' the historical narrative. But it could reasonably be said
that it is implicit also in the whole enterprise of the Fourth Gospel,
understood as our exegetes have seen it: as a narrative located

unmistakeably in the past of the world we inhabit, yet active upon us as the present challenge of God. I don't claim that the record of Anglican interpretation has been uniquely faithful to this and other traditions haven't; but there is more to the Westcott-inspired reading of history than an apologetic concern to save the appearances of historical plausibility in John's text. Some fairly fundamental principles are at stake.

Introduction

Chapter One

1. References to Tyndale's works are to the Parker Society edition, Cambridge, 1848.

Chapter Two

1. Quotations from Hooker are taken from R. Hooker, *The Works of That Learned and Judicious Divine Mr Richard Hooker* (3 vols; arr. J. Keble; 7th edn; rev. R.W. Church and F. Paget; Oxford: Clarendon Press, 1870).
2. 'The pit is ordinarily the end, as well of the guided as the guide in blindness', pp. 499–500.
3. 55 *passim*, pp. 238–45, 56. 6–7, pp. 248–51.
4. F.E. Hutchinson (ed.), *The Works of George Herbert* (Oxford: Clarendon Press, 2nd edn, 1945) pp. 200–1.
5. '[B]onds of obedience to God, strict obligations to the mutual exercise of Christian charity . . . warrants for the more security of our belief' and so on.
6. '[T]he very standing, rising and falling, the very steps and inflections every way', (pp. 159–60).
7. D. Shuger, ' "Societie Supernaturall": The Imagined Community of Hooker's Lawes', in A.C. McGrade (ed.), *Richard Hooker and the Construction of Christian Community* (Tempe: Medieval and Renaissance Texts and Studies 1997), pp. 307–29.
8. Shuger, 'Societie Supernaturall', pp. 324–5.
9. Shuger, 'Societie Supernaturall', p. 327.
10. Shuger, 'Societie Supernaturall', p. 323.
11. C. Condren, 'The Creation of Richard Hooker's Public Authority: Rhetoric, Reputation and Reassessment', *Journal of Religious History* 21.1 (1997), pp. 35–59.

Chapter Three

1. See, e.g., W.P. Jones, *Theological Worlds: Understanding the Alternative Rhythms of Christian Belief* (Nashville: Abingdon Press, 1989); Hans W. Frei, *Types of Christian Theology* (New Haven: Yale University Press, 1992).

2. Wesley A. Kort, *Bound to Differ: The Dynamics of Theological Discussion* (University Park: Pennsylvania State University Press, 1992).

3. Kort, pp. 101–4.

4. As in Proverbs 8:22ff., Job 28, Wisdom of Solomon 6:12–9:18.

5. I.16.8, cf. I.2.5 for an even more explicit allusion.

6. cf. V.8.1.

7. Printed by Keble as an appendix to *Laws V* under the title 'Answer to the Letter of certain English Protestants'. See especially section 28.

8. 'On the Certainty and Perpetuity of Faith in the Elect', Keble, vol. III, pp. 469–81 – an immensely important text in several ways in locating Hooker's doctrine of grace against its background.

9. Stanley Cavell, *The Claim of Reason: Wittgenstein, Skepticism, Morality and Tragedy* (Oxford: Clarendon Press, 1979); Martha Nussbaum, *The Fragility of Goodness: Luck and Ethics in Greek Tragedy and Philosophy* (Cambridge: Cambridge University Press, 1986).

10. Mary Hesse, *Models and Analogies in Science* (London: Sheed and Ward, 1963); (with Michael A. Arbib) *The Construction of Reality* (Cambridge: Cambridge University Press, 1986).

11. Roy Bhaskar, *The Possibility of Naturalism: A Philosophical Critique of the Contemporary Human Sciences* (Brighton: Harvester Press, 1979).

12. Bhaskar, *Philosophy and the Idea of Freedom* (Oxford: Basil Blackwell, 1991), p. 174.

13. See, e.g., I.7.6.

14. See, e.g., V.51.3; cf. Aquinas, *S. Th.* III.3.5 *ad* 2, III.7.1 *ad* 2, III.7.11 *ad* 1, III.23.3, etc.

15. See, e.g., III.10.

16. See III.10.6–7, 11.3ff.

17. III.10.5. The anticipation of Newman is striking.

18. See, e.g., VII.4.

19. See, e.g., I.10.2–4.

20. A former British Home Secretary (Kenneth Baker) was declared by the courts to have acted in contravention of the letter of the law in a case concerned with the deportation of an illegal immigrant. He was protected by the convention that the crown's ministers are in certain senses above the law. In comparable fashion, it has been claimed that the interest of the nation and the interest of the government of the day are one in law, so that there can be no appeal to the courts against what the government does to protect its interest; this was asserted at the time of the Clive Ponting trial in Britain, when a civil servant was prosecuted for breaking governmental security because of his belief that policies were being pursued contrary to the national interest.

21. cf. my paper 'Doctrinal Criticism: Some Questions' in Sarah Coakley and David Pailin (eds), *The Making and Remaking of Christian Doctrine: Essays in Honour of Maurice Wiles* (Oxford: Clarendon Press, 1993), pp. 239–64 esp. pp. 252–8.

Chapter Four

1. Elizabeth Clarke, *Theory and Theology in George Herbert's Poetry: 'Divinitie and Poesie, Met'*, (Oxford: Clarendon Press, 1997), pp. 272 ff. My debt to Clarke's analysis of Herbert will be obvious in what follows.
2. ibid., p. 52.
3. Keble, vol. I, p. 211.
4. Sermon II, Keble, Vol. III, pp. 483–547.
5. ibid., pp. 469–481.
6. ibid., p. 479.
7. ibid., pp. 471–2.
8. ibid., pp. 473–4.
9. ibid., p. 474.
10. ibid., p. 475.
11. *The Works of George Herbert*, ed. F.E. Hutchinson (Oxford: Clarendon Press, 1945), pp. 204–5.
12. Hooker, pp. 475–6.
13. Donald MacKinnon, 'Tillich, Frege, Kittel: Some Reflections on a Dark Theme', *Explorations in Theology* (London: SCM, 1979), pp. 129–137.

Chapter Five

1. A. Westcott, *Life and Letters of Brooke Foss Westcott*, vol. I (London: Macmillan, 1903), pp. 322–4.
2. ibid., p. 256.
3. Owen Chadwick, *The Victorian Church*, vol. II (London: A. & C. Black, 1970), p. 88.
4. ibid., p. 44.
5. ibid., p. 48.
6. Westcott, vol. II p. 72.
7. ibid., p. 85.
8. B.F. Westcott, *Lessons from Work* (London: Macmillan, 1901) p. 148.
9. C.f. Rowan Williams, 'Origen: Between Orthodoxy and Heresy', *Origeniana Septima*, ed. Wolfgang Bienert and Uwe Kühneweg (Leuven: Leuven University Press, 1999) pp. 3–14.
10. *Introduction to the Study of the Gospels* (London: Macmillan 2nd edn, 1851), p. 400; c.f. the letter of 21 July 1889 to Lady Welby, Westcott, vol. II, pp. 87–8.
11. To Lady Welby, 22 March 1886, Westcott, vol. II p. 84.
12. B.F. Westcott, *The Revelation of the Father* (London: Macmillan, 1884), p. 164.
13. B.F. Westcott, *The Gospel of St John* (London: John Murray, 1882), p. xliv.
14. Westcott, vol. I pp. 213–4.
15. Westcott, vol. II p. 81.
16. B.F. Westcott, *The Revelation of the Risen Lord* (London: Macmillan, 1881).
17. ibid., p. 52.
18. B.F. Westcott, *The Historic Faith* (London: Macmillan, 1883, and many times reprinted).

19. See the general introduction to the anthology of Anglican devotional writing, *Love's Redeeming Work*, ed. Geoffrey Rowell, Kenneth Stephenson and Rowan Williams (Oxford: Oxford University Press, 2001).
20. Westcott, vol. I pp. 52, 94.
21. ibid., p. 332.
22. ibid., p. 233.

Chapter Six

1. Michael Ramsey, *The Gospel and the Catholic Church* (London: Longman, 1936), p. 124 (henceforth *GCC*).
2. Don Cupitt, quoted in Michael De-la-Noy, *Michael Ramsey: A Portrait* (London: Fount, 1990), p. 99.
3. For reactions, see Owen Chadwick, *Michael Ramsey – A Life* (Oxford: Clarendon Press, 1990), pp. 48–50. For a very positive appraisal of *GCC*'s strengths in the context of its time, compare the brief remarks of Adrian Hastings, *A History of English Christianity, 1920–1985* (London: SCM Press, 1986), p. 261.
4. Readers may recall Dean Inge's reported comment when asked if he was interested in liturgy ('No. Neither do I collect postage stamps'), or A.C. Headlam's alleged judgement that, of all academic disciplines, those that most sapped the intellect were Hebrew and liturgiology.
5. John Milbank's *Theology and Social Theory* (Oxford: Basil Blackwell, 1990), represents the most systematic and original contribution to this debate from the theological world of late. See also the special issues of *New Blackfriars* (June 1992) and *Modern Theology* (October 1992) devoted to Milbank's book. For a wider spread of essays on religion and postmodernism, see Philippa Berry and Andrew Wernick (eds), *Shadow of Spirit: Post-Modernism and Religion* (London: Routledge, 1992).
6. For an excellent memoir of Hoskyns and a list of his works, see the introduction by Gordon Wakefield to the posthumously edited *Crucifixion–Resurrection: The Pattern of the Theology and Ethics of the New Testament*, E.C. Hoskyns and F.N. Davey (London: SPCK, 1981), pp. 27–81, and the bibliography, pp. 369–72.
7. *GCC*, pp. 169–71, 180, 181–93.
8. In this respect, he stands in sharp contrast to Gregory Dix, in some respects a kindred theological spirit; see, e.g., *The Shape of the Liturgy* (London: A & C Black, 1945), pp. 629–36, notably p. 636 ('Luther furnishes curious parallels with Adolf Hitler . . .'). The Methodist Gordon Rupp, whose earliest excursions into Luther scholarship were stimulated by comments comparable to those of Dix, was largely responsible for presenting to the British theological public a more balanced picture of Luther; in the 1960s, he and Ramsey shared a commitment to the ill-fated cause of Anglican–Methodist reunion. There would be an interesting essay to be written on the parallels between these two remarkable figures in whom the glib oppositions of Catholic and Protestant seemed to be overcome.
9. Richard Roberts, 'Theological rhetoric and moral passion in the light of

MacKinnon's "Barth"', in Kenneth Surin (ed.), *Christ, Ethics and Tragedy: Essays in Honour of Donald MacKinnon* (Cambridge: Cambridge University Press, 1989), pp. 1–14 (e.g. p. 12).

10. ibid., p. 12 ('an ecclesiological impossibilism grounded at least in part in an appropriation of dialectical theology').

11. *GCC*, pp. 210ff.

12. Despite the quotation on p. 212 ('The death of Christ is actually, literally, the death of you and me'), Maurice seems more concerned to make a point about our recognition of the illusoriness of the isolated self than to elaborate a pedagogy of the cross. We should also note the difference between Maurice's and Barth's repudiation of 'religion'. Maurice rejects 'religion' as a separate sphere of culture and polity, Barth as the human attempt to domesticate God in culture and polity.

13. Some of the material from *GCC* is reproduced pretty much as it stands in Michael Ramsey (ed. Dale Coleman), *The Anglican Spirit* (London: SPCK, 1991), pp. 69–77.

14. See, e.g., David Nicholls and Rowan Williams, *Politics and Theological Identity* (London: Jubilee Group, 1984).

15. *GCC* has two references to Georges Vasilievich Florovsky on ecclesiology; the middle 1930s marked the beginnings of Florovsky's influence in the ecumenical movement, and of his regular visits to English and Scottish theological institutions. He met Ramsey during the latter's time at Lincoln, and they remained friends. See Andrew Blane (ed.), *Georges Florovsky: Russian Intellectual, Orthodox Churchman* (Crestwood, NY: St Vladimir's Seminary Press, 1993), p. 69, with n81 on p. 186, and n230 on p. 205.

16. *GCC*, p. 197.

17. ibid., p. 172.

18. ibid., pp. 198–201; and see p. 120 on the mirror image of the failures of Catholicism and Protestantism.

19. ibid., p. 28.

20. ibid., p. 118.

21. ibid., p. 73.

22. There is a venerable Anglican tradition behind this, perhaps most eloquently set out in Jeremy Taylor's *The Worthy Communicant*; see, e.g., the text quoted in Thomas K. Carroll (ed.), *Jeremy Taylor: Selected Works* (New York/Mahwah, NJ: Paulist Press, 1990), pp. 209ff.

23. In addition to Florovsky's work, Ramsey would probably have read Sergei Bulgakov, *The Orthodox Church* (London: Centenary Press, 1935); ch. 3 of this work sets out a theology of 'hierarchy' in terms of the 'charismatic power' to transmit the grace of the sacraments, quite distinct from any power to rule over the laity as subjects, which would be destructive of the sense of interdependent charisms in the one Church. In addition, the closeness of Ramsey's vision to that of John Zizioulas, in more recent Orthodox thought, is striking; see, in particular, chs 5 and 6 of Zizioulas' *Being As Communion* (London: Darton, Longman and Todd, 1985).

24. Two relevant (though very different) books in this connection are Donald

Davidson's influential collection, *Inquiries into Truth and Interpretation* (Oxford: Oxford University Press, 1984), and Fergus Kerr, *Theology after Wittgenstein* (Oxford: Basil Blackwell, 1986). Both defend varieties of realism (language has a relation to what is not language, and is in some significant measure determined by what is not language) while demonstrating that a theory of language as the naming of discrete lumps of experienced reality is philosophically unsustainable.

25. *GCC*, p. 121.
26. ibid., pp. 121–4.
27. Ch. 2 of *Being As Communion* (see n23 above); cf. Florovsky's essay, 'Revelation, Philosophy, and Theology' (originally published in German in 1931) in *Creation and Redemption*, vol. 3 of the Collected Works of Georges Florovsky (Belmont, Mass.: Nordland Publishing Co, 1976), pp. 21–40.
28. *Being As Communion*, pp. 114–22.
29. See ch. 3.
30. For the text of Ramsey's remarks in his presidential address to the Convocation of Canterbury in May 1963, in which he expressed some criticism of *Honest to God*, see Eric James, *A Life of Bishop John A.T. Robinson: Scholar, Pastor, Prophet* (London: Fount, 1987), pp. 120–1. His booklet, *Image Old and New*, published a little earlier, had set out more sympathetically and fully some of his reactions.
31. Michael De-la-Noy, *Michael Ramsey*, pp. 100, 194–6, quoting a variety of contemporary theologians.
32. See, e.g., the very powerful and often moving works of Graham Shaw, *The Cost of Authority* (London: SCM Press, 1983), and *God in our Hands* (London: SCM Press, 1987); and studies of the patristic period such as those of Elaine Pagels, *The Gnostic Gospels* (London: Penguin, 1980); *Adam, Eve and the Serpent* (London: Penguin, 1988)).
33. *GCC*, p. 180.
34. I have tried to elaborate this a little in 'Imagining the Kingdom: some questions for Anglican worship today' in Kenneth Stevenson and Brian Spinks (eds), *The Identity of Anglican Worship* (London: Mowbray, 1991), pp. 1–13.
35. *Letters and Papers from Prison. The Enlarged Edition* (London: SCM Press, 1971), p. 300.

Chapter Seven

1. Adrian Hastings, *A History of English Christianity 1920–1990*, 3rd edn (London: SCM Press, 1991), p. 537.
2. In preface to Alasdair MacIntyre, *Marxism and Christianity*, revised edn (London: Duckworth, 1969), p. 7.
3. ibid., p. 8.
4. David L. Edwards (ed.), *The Honest to God Debate* (London: SCM Press, 1963), p. 215.
5. ibid., p. 217.
6. ibid., p. 221.

7. ibid., p. 222.
8. ibid., p. 222.
9. ibid., p. 230.
10. John A. T. Robinson, *Honest to God* (London: SCM Press, 1963), p. 49.
11. ibid., p. 53.
12. See, e.g., ibid., p. 29–30.
13. Edwards, *The Honest to God Debate*, p. 195.
14. Robinson, *Honest to God*, p. 99.
15. Austin Marsden Farrer, *Finite and Infinite: A Philosophical Essay* (London: Dacre Press, 1949; 2nd edn, 1959).
16. E.L. Mascall, *Christ, the Christian and the Church: A Study of the Incarnation and its Consequences* (London: Darton, Longman & Todd, 1946).
17. Werner and Lotte Pelz, *God Is No More* (London: Gollancz, 1963).
18. ibid., p. 119.
19. ibid., p. 37.
20. ibid., p. 78–81.
21. ibid., p. 131–8.
22. ibid., p. 14.
23. Robinson, *Honest to God*, p. 115.
24. John A.T. Robinson, *Exploration Into God* (London: SCM Press, 1967).
25. Gareth Moore, *Believing in God: A Philosophical Essay* (Edinburgh: T & T Clark, 1988), p. 279.
26. Herbert McCabe, in *The Honest to God Debate*, p. 166.
27. Donald M. MacKinnon, 'Tillich, Frege, Kittel: Some Reflections on a Dark Theme', *Explorations in Theology* 5 (London: SCM Press, 1979), p. 135.
28. See Robert Towler, *The Need for Certainty: A Sociological Study of Conventional Religion*, International Library of Sociology (London: Routledge & Kegan Paul, 1984).

Chapter Eight

1. B.F. Westcott, *The Gospel of St John* (London: John Murray, 1882).
2. ibid., pp. xlix–l.
3. ibid., p. lv.
4. ibid., p. lxxiv.
5. E.C. Hoskyns, *The Fourth Gospel* (London: Faber, 1940).
6. Davey's preface (pp. 7–10 in particular) summarises the process of composition.
7. ibid., p. 85.
8. ibid., pp. 81–2.
9. ibid., p. 117 (italics in original).
10. ibid., pp. 114.
11. ibid., p. 118.
12. ibid., p. 123; pp. 120–3 overall develop the point about the 'end' as articulated and made present only in the Spirit, not in either straightforward historical narrative or simply speculative form.
13. ibid., p. 127.

14. ibid., p. 132.
15. William Temple, *Readings in St John's Gospel*, originally published in two series, 1939 and 1940, then as one volume in 1945 (London: Macmillan). References here are to the one volume edition.
16. ibid., p. xiii.
17. ibid., p. xvii.
18. ibid., pp. xvii–xviii.
19. ibid., p. xx ff.
20. ibid., p. 114.
21. ibid., p. 98.
22. ibid., p. 92.
23. ibid., p. 231.
24. J.A.T. Robinson, *The Priority of John*, ed. J.F. Coakley (London: SCM, 1985).
25. ibid., pp. 302–3.
26. ibid., pp. 312–5.
27. ibid., p. 327.
28. ibid., p. 328.
29. ibid., pp. 329–39.
30. ibid., p. 345.
31. ibid., pp. 345–6.
32. ibid., p. 352.
33. See Piet Schoonenberg, *The Christ* (London: Sheed and Ward, 1972).

INDEX